Good Housekeeping

The Complete
Household
Organizer

Hearst Books

A Division of Sterling Publishing Co., Inc.

New York

GOOD HOUSEKEEPING
Rosemary Ellis • Editor in Chief
Richard Eisenberg • Special Projects Director

THE GOOD HOUSEKEEPING RESEARCH INSTITUTE
John Kupsch • P.E. Technical Director
Carolyn E. Forté • Home Care Director/Associate
    Institute Director
Sharon Franke • Food Appliances Director
Delia Hammock, M.S., R.D.
Kathleen Huddy Sperduto • Textiles Director
Stacy Genovese • Engineering Director
Karen Rauen, Ph.D. • Chemistry Director

PROJECT EDITOR
Susan Randol

BOOK DESIGN by Elizabeth Van Italie

COVER PHOTOS
Upper left corner • Bruce Buck
Upper center • Courtesy of KraftMaid Cabinetry,
    800-571-1990, www.kraftmaid.com
Bottom center • Courtesy of Rubbermaid,
    888-895-2110, www.rubbermaid.com

INTERIOR PHOTOS
Safety & Health tab • Emily Wilson
Family Life tab • ©Royalty-Free/Corbis
Cleaning and Clothing Care tab • Michael Kraus
Decorating tab • Matthew Millman
Vacations, Celebrations, and Entertaining tab •
    ©Peter Mason/Getty Images
Maintenance and Repair tab •
    ©Susi Bikle/iStockphoto
Garden and Yard tab • Rob Cardillo
Finances tab • Stephen Webster
Car tab • Courtesy of Ford Motor Company

Library of Congress Cataloging-in-Publication Data
Good housekeeping : the complete household
organizer / by the editors of Good housekeeping.
    p.cm.
Includes index.
ISBN 1-58816-558-2
1. Home economics. I. Title: Complete household
organizer. II. Good housekeeping.

TX147.G645 2006
640—dc22   2005019135

10 9 8 7 6 5

Published by Hearst Books
A Division of Sterling Publishing Co., Inc.
387 Park Avenue South, New York, NY 10016

Good Housekeeping and Hearst Books are
trademarks of Hearst Communications, Inc.

www.goodhousekeeping.com

For information about custom editions, special sales, premium and corporate purchases, please contact Sterling Special Sales Department at 800-805-5489 or specialsales@sterlingpub.com.

Distributed in Canada by Sterling Publishing
c/o Canadian Manda Group, 165 Dufferin Street
Toronto, Ontario, Canada M6K 3H6

Distributed in Australia by Capricorn Link
(Australia) Pty. Ltd.
P.O. Box 704, Windsor, NSW 2756 Australia

Manufactured in China

Sterling ISBN 13: 978-1-58816-558-9
        ISBN 10: 1-58816-558-2

The Complete
Household
Organizer

Table of Contents

Foreword

I consider myself to be a pretty organized person. But here's a confession: until recently, some of the most important information about our home and family was a bit scattered. Then I read the household organizer you're holding, and I got smart. With this helpful guide, I now have in one place everything from our plumber's phone number to the measurements of our living room windows. It's hard to remember how I managed without *Good Housekeeping: The Complete Household Organizer*! Once you put it to use, I bet you'll wonder how you ever kept your home running, too.

For detailed advice about maintaining, decorating, and improving your home, I strongly recommend the companion book to this organizer: *Good Housekeeping: The Complete Household Handbook*. And the Good Housekeeping website, www.goodhousekeeping.com, offers more useful tips and checklists to help make your home everything you want it to be.

Managing a household can be tricky and frustrating. But I think you'll find that this household organizer will help make the process less stressful and save you time. Then you'll be able to spend more hours enjoying your home.

Ellen Levine
Editor in Chief
Good Housekeeping

Introduction

Are you tired of searching your house for the plumber's phone number? Did you forget when the mortgage payment was due? Or when your car needs an oil change? Or when you need to schedule your next dental appointment?

If you're like most people running a household, you've had moments like these—or worse! That's why the experts at the Good Housekeeping Research Institute have created this invaluable home organizer that helps you keep track of all the information necessary to run a household smoothly. Divided into sections devoted to specific aspects of running a house, *Good Housekeeping: The Complete Household Organizer* is filled with pages that let you record vital information about your safety and health; your family life; cleaning and clothing care; decorating; vacations, celebrations, and entertaining; home maintenance and repair; your garden and yard; your finances; and your car.

This complete organizer even includes a handy pocket in each section where you can store bits and pieces of paper and other information that normally migrates to different places in your house—receipts, warranties, business cards, paint chips, and so on.

Once you finish filling in the pages, you'll be able to find all the information you need at a moment's notice. Don't forget to use a pencil for the information that will be updated on a routine basis, such as school teachers. You can photocopy blank pages, fill them out every year, and keep the completed pages in the pocket of the relevant section. You may also want to photo-copy sections to carry with you, such as the list of car pool participants to keep in the glove compartment of your car.

The end of the organizer features pages for you to record all your account numbers and passwords—from your debit card to your frequent flyer PIN—so you won't have to hunt them down when you need them. For security purposes, you should tear out these pages and keep them in a separate, secure place.

We've based this organizer on a family with three children, but have included blank space at the end of each section so you can record additional information if you have more than three youngsters. This notes section is handy for recording other information specific to your family, or for writing down information—measurements for additional windows in the decorating chapter, for example—that isn't covered in that particular section.

The experts at the Good Housekeeping Research Institute have also added useful hints and tips throughout the organizer. You'll find their advice on matters like what to keep in your car for an emergency; how to decipher fabric-care symbols; and how to find a doctor when you're on vacation. The Good Housekeeping Research Institute, which has tested and evaluated thousands of household products and offered invaluable advice to consumers for more than 100 years, is also responsible for the administration of the Good Housekeeping Seal, the nationally recognized logo for products backed by a limited warranty from *Good Housekeeping* magazine.

If you're looking to centralize all the information that has been floating around your house for years, hoping to keep the myriad household details in one place (other than in your head), and dreaming of the day when you only have to turn a few pages to uncover the information you need, this household organizer is for you. So sharpen your pencil, open this book, and get started on a new, more organized you!

—The Editors of *Good Housekeeping*

Safety and Health

Safety and Health

Use this section to record vital information about your family's safety and health: contact information for doctors, insurance companies, police, and hospitals; phone numbers for your utility companies in case of emergency; purchase and maintenance information on household safety devices like carbon monoxide detectors; your family's emergency plans; and much more. You can use the pocket to store eyeglass prescriptions, business cards for medical professionals, school memos regarding emergency evacuation plans, copies of your insurance cards—even copies of immunization histories. Here's the place and now's the time to start recording information that will keep your family safe and well.

Safety ☎

CONTACT INFORMATION

PERSONAL SAFETY

ALARM SYSTEM COMPANY: _____

    Phone number: _____

    Address: _____

    Name of friend with alarm information and password for alarm company: _____

    _____

    Phone number: _____

AMBULANCE: _____

    Emergency: 911

    Non-emergency phone number: _____

FIRE DEPARTMENT: _____

    Emergency: 911

    Non-emergency phone number: _____

HOSPITAL: _____

    Phone number: _____

    Address: _____

EMERGENCY ROOM OR NOT?

It's happened to all of us: you meant to cut the cucumber, but you cut your hand instead. Do you wash your hand and bandage it, or do you head to the emergency room? If any of the following apply, either call your doctor or go directly to the emergency room:

➤ The cut is big or deep. Any cut longer than an inch is emergency room material.

➤ You've put steady pressure on the cut, but bleeding doesn't stop within 15 minutes.

➤ The cut or puncture was caused by a rusty object.

➤ The area becomes increasingly red or painful or you notice a yellow discharge.

➤ The general area feels numb, hurts, or feels weak when you move it. You may have caused nerve or tendon damage, so head to the hospital right away.

➤ You have not had a tetanus shot within the last ten years.

POISON CONTROL CENTER: _____

    Emergency: 800-222-1222

    Local phone number: _____

POLICE: _____

    Emergency: 911

    Non-emergency phone number:_____

UTILITIES

ELECTRIC COMPANY: _____

    Emergency phone number: _____

    Customer service phone number: _____

    24-hour service phone number: _____

    Account number: _____

GAS COMPANY: _____

    Emergency phone number: _____

    Customer service phone number: _____

    24-hour service phone number: _____

    Account number: _____

OIL COMPANY: _____

    Emergency phone number: _____

    Customer service phone number: _____

    24-hour service phone number: _____

    Account number: _____

WATER COMPANY: _____

    Emergency phone number: _____

    Customer service phone number: _____

    24-hour service phone number: _____

    Account number: _____

EMERGENCY CONTACT INFORMATION

People to contact in an emergency:

Name: _____

Relationship: _____

Home phone number: _____

Work phone number: _____

Cell phone number: _____

Address: _____

Name: _____

Relationship: _____

Home phone number: _____

Work phone number: _____

Cell phone number: _____

Address: _____

Name: _____

Relationship: _____

Home phone number: _____

Work phone number: _____

Cell phone number: _____

Address: _____

SAFETY EQUIPMENT

CARBON MONOXIDE DETECTOR

Location: _____

Date purchased: _____ Date batteries were changed: _____

CARBON MONOXIDE DETECTOR

Location: _____

Date purchased: _____ Date batteries were changed: _____

CARBON MONOXIDE DETECTOR

Location: _____

Date purchased: _____ Date batteries were changed: _____

FIRE EXTINGUISHER

Location: _____

Purchased from: _____ Date: _____

Warranty (yes/no)? _____Date of expiration: _____

FIRE EXTINGUISHER

Location: _____

Purchased from: _____ Date: _____

Warranty (yes/no)? _____Date of expiration: _____

SMOKE DETECTOR

Location: _____

Warranty (yes/no)? _____Date batteries were changed: _____

SMOKE DETECTOR

Location: _____

Date purchased: _____ Date batteries were changed: _____

SMOKE DETECTOR

Location: _____

Date purchased: _____ Date batteries were changed: _____

TIME TO CHANGE

Want an easy way to remember when you should replace the batteries in your smoke detectors? Put in new batteries twice a year: once when you switch to daylight savings time in the spring, and once when you switch back in the fall.

NIGHTTIME SAFETY

Make your emergency plans during the day, but practice your fire drills at night. According to a National Safe Kids report, 50 percent of fire deaths occur at night—between 11 PM and 6 AM.

EMERGENCY PLANS

Your world may be in flux, but you need cast-in-stone emergency plans for your family. Decide on two specific meeting places outside your house: one a safe distance from your house in case of an emergency like a fire, and one outside your neighborhood in case you can't return home. Be sure to confirm these plans with every family member. Don't forget to also record the name and phone number of an out-of-state relative or friend every family member should call if local phones don't work in an emergency. Use this relative or friend to pass along messages to family members.

MEETING PLACE NEAR HOUSE

Location: _____

Address: _____

Phone number: _____

MEETING PLACE OUTSIDE NEIGHBORHOOD

Location: _____

Address: _____

Phone number: _____

OUT-OF-STATE EMERGENCY CONTACT

Name: _____

Phone number: _____

Cell phone number: _____

Health✚

CONTACT INFORMATION

MEDICAL

ALLERGIST: _____

Medical group: _____

Other doctors in the practice: _____

Phone number: _____ Fax number: _____

Address: _____

E-mail address: _____

Hospital affiliation: _____

Phone number: _____

Address: _____

Date of visit: _____

DERMATOLOGIST: _____

Medical group: _____

Other doctors in the practice: _____

Phone number: _____ Fax number: _____

Address: _____

E-mail address: _____

Hospital affiliation: _____

Phone number: _____

Address: _____

Date of visit: _____

GENERAL PRACTITIONER: _____

Medical group: _____

Other doctors in the practice: _____

Phone number: _____ Fax number: _____

Address: _____

E-mail address: _____

Hospital affiliation: _____

Phone number: _____

Address: _____

Date of visit: _____

GENERAL PRACTITIONER: _____

Medical group: _____

Other doctors in the practice: _____

Phone number: _____ Fax number: _____

Address: _____

E-mail address: _____

Hospital affiliation: _____

   Phone number: _____

   Address: _____

Date of visit: _____

OB/GYN: _____

   Medical group: _____

    Other doctors in the practice: _____

   Phone number: _____ Fax number: _____

   Address: _____

   E-mail address: _____

   Hospital affiliation: _____

    Phone number: _____

    Address: _____

   Date of visit: _____

   Date of mammogram: _____ Place: _____

    Phone number: _____

    Address: _____

OPTOMETRIST/OPHTHALMOLOGIST (ADULT): _____

   Medical group: _____

    Other doctors in the practice: _____

HEALTHY EYES

Follow these four guidelines to keep your eyes in tip-top shape:

➤ If you have vision problems, have an eye exam every two years until you're 40. After 40, everyone (those with problems and those without) should have an eye exam every two years. An optometrist can perform the exam unless your family has a history of eye disease—in that case, make sure you see an ophthalmologist.

➤ Don't smoke. Smoking increases your chances of developing cataracts and age-related macular degeneration, which destroys central vision.

➤ Make sure your sunglasses give you 100 percent ultraviolet protection.

➤ Eat your vegetables—dark green leafy vegetables, to be precise. They contain lutein, which may decrease your risk of age-related macular degeneration.

Phone number: _____ _____ Fax number: _____

Address: _____

E-mail address: _____

Hospital affiliation: _____

Phone number: _____

Address: _____

Date of visit: _____

OPTOMETRIST/OPHTHALMOLOGIST (PEDIATRIC): _____

Medical group: _____

Other doctors in the practice: _____

Phone number: _____ Fax number: _____

Address: _____

E-mail address: _____

Hospital affiliation: _____

Phone number: _____

Address: _____

Date of visit: _____

PEDIATRICIAN: _____

Medical group: _____

Other doctors in the practice: _____

Phone number: _____ Fax number: _____

Address: _____

E-mail address: _____

Hospital affiliation: _____

Phone number: _____

Address: _____

Date of visit: _____

SCHOOL NURSE: *See Family Life, page 27.*

OTHER: _____

  Medical group: _____

    Other doctors in the practice: _____

  Phone number: _____ Fax number: _____

  Address: _____

  E-mail address: _____

  Hospital affiliation: _____

    Phone number: _____

    Address: _____

  Date of visit: _____

OTHER: _____

  Medical group: _____

    Other doctors in the practice: _____

  Phone number: _____ Fax number: _____

  Address: _____

  E-mail address: _____

  Hospital affiliation: _____

    Phone number: _____

    Address: _____

  Date of visit: _____

OTHER: _____

  Medical group: _____

    Other doctors in the practice: _____

  Phone number: _____ Fax number: _____

  Address: _____

  E-mail address: _____

  Hospital affiliation: _____

    Phone number: _____

    Address: _____

  Date of visit: _____

OTHER: _____

    Medical group: _____

      Other doctors in the practice: _____

    Phone number: _____ Fax number: _____

    Address: _____

    E-mail address: _____

    Hospital affiliation: _____

      Phone number: _____

      Address: _____

    Date of visit: _____

DENTAL

DENTIST (ADULT): _____

    Dental group: _____

      Other dentists in the practice: _____

    Phone number: _____ Fax number: _____

    Address: _____

    E-mail address: _____

    Date of visit: _____

DENTIST (PEDIATRIC): _____

    Dental group: _____

      Other dentists in the practice: _____

    Phone number: _____ Fax number: _____

    Address: _____

FLOSS FOR HEALTH

Don't know which kind of dental floss to use? Simply choose whichever one you find most comfortable. You can also keep these guidelines in mind:

➤ Try narrow, waxed dental floss if your teeth are close together.

➤ Use unwaxed floss for teeth with room between them.

➤ Consider dental tape if your teeth are spaced widely apart.

➤ Floss with prethreaded, disposable floss holders if you have trouble using traditional dental floss.

E-mail address: _____

Date of visit: _____

ORTHODONTIST: _____

Dental group: _____

Other orthodontists in the practice: _____

Phone number: _____ Fax number: _____

Address: _____

E-mail address: _____

Date of visit: _____

OTHER: _____

Dental group: _____

Other specialists in the practice: _____

Phone number: _____ Fax number: _____

Address: _____

E-mail address: _____

Date of visit: _____

OTHER: _____

Dental group: _____

Other specialists in the practice: _____

Phone number: _____ Fax number: _____

Address: _____

E-mail address: _____

Date of visit: _____

INSURANCE INFORMATION

MEDICAL INSURANCE

Name of insurer: _____

Name of health plan: _____

Primary cardholder: _____

Group number: _____

Member number: _____

ID numbers: _____

_____

Customer service phone number: _____

Address for submitting claims: _____

Annual deductible: _____Copay: _____

Copay for specialist: _____Copay for alternative medicine: _____

Referral needed (yes/no)? _____

DENTAL INSURANCE

Name of insurer: _____

Name of dental plan: _____

Primary cardholder: _____

Group number: _____

Member number: _____

ID numbers: _____

_____

Customer service phone number: _____

Address for submitting claims: _____

Annual deductible: _____

Percent reimbursed: _____

Referral needed (yes/no)? _____

PRESCRIPTION MEDICINE

PHARMACY: _____

Pharmacist: _____

Phone number: _____

Address: _____

Hours: _____

24-HOUR PHARMACY: _____

Pharmacist: _____

Phone number: _____

Address: _____

MAIL-ORDER PHARMACY: _____

Phone number: _____

Address: _____

Password: _____

PRESCRIPTION KEPT AT PHARMACY: _____

Name of pharmacy: _____

Refill date: _____

PRESCRIPTION KEPT AT PHARMACY: _____

Name of pharmacy: _____

Refill date: _____

PRESCRIPTION KEPT AT PHARMACY: _____

Name of pharmacy: _____

Refill date: _____

PRESCRIPTION KEPT AT PHARMACY: _____

Name of pharmacy: _____

Refill date: _____

PRESCRIPTION KEPT AT PHARMACY: _____

Name of pharmacy: _____

Refill date: _____

ALLERGY INFORMATION

NAME: _____

    Allergies: _____

    Medications: _____

NAME: _____

    Allergies: _____

    Medications: _____

NAME: _____

    Allergies: _____

    Medications: _____

NAME: _____

    Allergies: _____

    Medications: _____

NAME: _____

    Allergies: _____

    Medications: _____

EXERCISE

HEALTH CLUB/GYM: _____

    Phone number: _____ Fax number: _____

    Address: _____

    E-mail address: _____

    Membership number: _____

    Initial cost: _____ Monthly payment:_____

    Method of payment: _____

EXORCISE THE GUILT

Don't feel guilty if you can't squeeze in a 30-minute workout during the day. A recent study showed that exercising three times a day for ten minutes each time was more effective than a 30-minute session in lowering fat and triglyceride levels.

HEALTH CLUB/GYM: _____

    Phone number: _____ Fax number: _____

    Address: _____

    E-mail address: _____

    Membership number: _____

    Initial cost: _____ Monthly payment:_____

    Method of payment: _____

Notes

_____

_____

_____

_____

_____

_____

_____

_____

_____

_____

_____

_____

_____

_____

_____

_____

_____

_____

_____

_____

_____

Family Life

Family Life

The old saying, "The devil is in the details," is perhaps most true when you're talking about the endless amount of information you need to make sure each day runs smoothly for you and your family. It's not easy keeping straight the cost of your child's lunch, the phone number of the veterinarian, and your spouse's shirt size. That's why this section leaves plenty of space for all those details: contact information for teachers, coaches, car pools, haircutters, dog walkers, and others—plus checklists for clothing and shoe sizes and tables to help you remember important school dates. So grab a pencil and all those bits of paper scattered around your house that keep life moving forward, and make this section the key to a smooth family life. Don't forget that you can keep business cards, notes from school, lists of online purchases, school class lists, and coupons in the pocket.

School, After-school Activities, and Camp

SCHOOL CONTACT INFORMATION

NAME OF CHILD: _____

Name of school: _____

    Phone number: _____

    Address: _____

Principal: _____

    Phone number: _____ E-mail address: _____

Assistant Principal/Office secretary: _____

    Phone number: _____ E-mail address: _____

Homeroom teacher: _____

    Phone number: _____ E-mail address: _____

Class parent: _____

    Phone number: _____ Cell phone number: _____

    E-mail address: _____

Teacher: _____

    Phone number: _____ E-mail address: _____

Teacher: _____

    Phone number: _____ E-mail address: _____

Teacher: _____

    Phone number: _____ E-mail address: _____

THE PERFECT GIFT

You want to give your child's teacher an end-of-the-year gift to thank her for all she's done for your child, but you don't know what's appropriate—or even have any ideas. Here are some tried-and-true gift ideas, including some suggested by teachers themselves:
- Stationery
- Gift certificates (to bookstores, restaurants, department stores, specialty stores)
- Movie passes
- Fruit baskets
- Baked goods

Teacher: _____

    Phone number: _____ E-mail address: _____

Teacher: _____

    Phone number: _____ E-mail address: _____

Teacher: _____

    Phone number: _____ E-mail address: _____

Guidance Counseler: _____

    Phone number: _____ E-mail address: _____

School Nurse: _____

    Phone number: _____ E-mail address: _____

PTA contact: _____

    Phone number: _____ E-mail address: _____

Transportation (bus company): _____

  Supervisor: _____

    Phone number: _____ E-mail address: _____

  Bus driver: _____

  Bus number: _____

  Bus monitor: _____

    Cell phone number: _____

Tutor: _____

    Phone number: _____ Cell phone number: _____

    Address: _____

    E-mail address: _____

    Day/time of lesson: _____ Cost: _____

After-school child care: _____

    Phone number: _____ E-mail address: _____

    Address: _____

    Cost: _____

NAME OF CHILD: _____

Name of school: _____

Phone number: _____

Address: _____

Principal: _____

Phone number: _____ E-mail address: _____

Assistant Principal/Office secretary: _____

Phone number: _____ E-mail address: _____

Homeroom teacher: _____

Phone number: _____ E-mail address: _____

Class parent: _____

Phone number: _____ Cell phone number: _____

E-mail address: _____

Teacher: _____

Phone number: _____ E-mail address: _____

Teacher: _____

Phone number: _____ E-mail address: _____

Teacher: _____

Phone number: _____ E-mail address: _____

Teacher: _____

Phone number: _____ E-mail address: _____

Teacher: _____

Phone number: _____ E-mail address: _____

Teacher: _____

Phone number: _____ E-mail address: _____

Guidance Counseler: _____

Phone number: _____ E-mail address: _____

School Nurse: _____

Phone number: _____ E-mail address: _____

PTA contact: _____

Phone number: _____ E-mail address: _____

Transportation (bus company): _____

Supervisor: _____

    Phone number: _____ E-mail address: _____

Bus driver: _____

Bus number: _____

Bus monitor: _____

    Cell phone number: _____

Tutor: _____

    Phone number: _____ Cell phone number: _____

    Address: _____

    E-mail address: _____

    Day/time of lesson: _____ Cost: _____

After-school child care: _____

    Phone number: _____ E-mail address: _____

    Address: _____

    Cost: _____

NAME OF CHILD: _____

Name of school: _____

    Phone number: _____

    Address: _____

Principal: _____

    Phone number: _____ E-mail address: _____

Assistant Principal/Office secretary: _____

    Phone number: _____ E-mail address: _____

Homeroom teacher: _____

    Phone number: _____ E-mail address: _____

Class parent: _____

    Phone number: _____ Cell phone number: _____

    E-mail address: _____

Teacher: _____

    Phone number: _____ E-mail address: _____

Teacher: _____

Phone number: _____ E-mail address: _____

Teacher: _____

Phone number: _____ E-mail address: _____

Teacher: _____

Phone number: _____ E-mail address: _____

Teacher: _____

Phone number: _____ E-mail address: _____

Teacher: _____

Phone number: _____ E-mail address: _____

Guidance Counseler: _____

Phone number: _____ E-mail address: _____

School Nurse: _____

Phone number: _____ E-mail address: _____

PTA contact: _____

Phone number: _____ E-mail address: _____

Transportation (bus company): _____

Supervisor: _____

Phone number: _____ E-mail address: _____

Bus driver: _____

Bus number: _____

Bus monitor: _____

Cell phone number: _____

Tutor: _____

Phone number: _____ Cell phone number: _____

Address: _____

E-mail address: _____

Day/time of lesson: _____ Cost: _____

After-school child care: _____

    Phone number: _____ E-mail address: _____

    Address: _____

    Cost: _____

PLAYGROUND SAFETY

Parents who plan ahead and pay attention at playgrounds are parents who keep their children safe, according to a recent study. Here's what parents can do:

➤ Remove all hoods and drawstrings from your children's clothes, and don't let them wear necklaces or scarves.

➤ Make sure the play equipment is age-appropriate for your particular child.

➤ Check out the surface under the equipment; avoid playgrounds that have concrete or asphalt surfaces.

➤ Dress your children appropriately for the elements—rain, wind, heat, or cold.

➤ Stay close and pay attention to what your child is doing.

AFTER-SCHOOL ACTIVITIES CONTACT INFORMATION

ART LESSON

Name of child: _____

Type of art: _____

Day of lesson: _____

    Time: _____

    Location: _____

Teacher: _____

    Phone number: _____ Cell phone number: _____

    E-mail address: _____

DANCE LESSON

Name of child: _____

Type of dance: _____

Day of lesson: _____

    Time: _____

    Location: _____

Teacher: _____

    Phone number: _____ Cell phone number: _____

    E-mail address: _____

MUSIC LESSON

Name of child: _____

Instrument: _____

Day of lesson: _____

    Time: _____

    Location: _____

Teacher: _____

    Phone number: _____ Cell phone number: _____

    E-mail address: _____

Instrument rental/Music store: _____

    Phone number: _____ E-mail address: _____

    Address: _____

    Cost: _____ Renewal date: _____

MUSIC LESSON

Name of child: _____

Instrument: _____

Day of lesson: _____

    Time: _____

    Location: _____

Teacher: _____

    Phone number: _____ Cell phone number: _____

    E-mail address: _____

Instrument rental/Music store: _____

    Phone number: _____ E-mail address: _____

    Address: _____

    Cost: _____ Renewal date: _____

MUSIC LESSON

Name of child: _____

Instrument: _____

Day of lesson: _____

    Time: _____

    Location: _____

Teacher: _____

    Phone number: _____ Cell phone number: _____

    E-mail address: _____

Instrument rental/Music store: _____

    Phone number: _____ E-mail address: _____

    Address: _____

    Cost: _____ Renewal date: _____

PIANO TUNER: *See Maintenance and Repair, page 112.*

RELIGIOUS INSTRUCTION

Name of child: _____

Day of instruction: _____

    Time: _____

    Location: _____

Teacher: _____

    Phone number: _____ Cell phone number: _____

    E-mail address: _____

RELIGIOUS INSTRUCTION

Name of child: _____

Day of instruction: _____

    Time: _____

    Location: _____

Teacher: _____

    Phone number: _____ Cell phone number: _____

    E-mail address: _____

RELIGIOUS INSTRUCTION

Name of child: _____

Day of instruction: _____

    Time: _____

    Location: _____

Teacher: _____

    Phone number: _____ Cell phone number: _____

    E-mail address: _____

SPORT: _____

Name of child: _____

Name of team: _____

Day(s) of practice: _____

    Time: _____

    Location: _____

Coach: _____

    Phone number: _____ Cell phone number: _____

    E-mail address: _____

Coach: _____

    Phone number: _____ Cell phone number: _____

    E-mail address: _____

SPORT: _____

Name of child: _____

Name of team: _____

Day(s) of practice: _____

    Time: _____

    Location: _____

Coach: _____

    Phone number: _____ Cell phone number: _____

    E-mail address: _____

Coach: _____

SAVINGS ON SPORTS GEAR

Although some lucky parents have children who play sports that don't require a lot of equipment, others find themselves having to buy endless amounts of sports gear year after year. There are alternatives, however, to ending up in the poorhouse:

➤ Check out annual gear swaps held by local sports organizations.

➤ Find retailers who sell secondhand sports equipment. Make sure that the equipment is in good condition—that there are no cracks or pieces missing.

➤ Take advantage of the Internet: Some sites sell used sports gear. Again, confirm that the equipment is in proper shape.

➤ Call sports stores that specialize in one sport; many have a trade-in program. Bicycle repair shops and retailers often have this type of program, for example, and the bikes they sell have been refurbished and professionally road tested.

➤ Safety and protective gear—such as helmets, eyewear, and undergarment padding—should not be bought secondhand.

Phone number: _____ Cell phone number: _____

E-mail address: _____

SPORT: _____

Name of child: _____

Name of team: _____

Day(s) of practice: _____

Time: _____

Location: _____

Coach: _____

Phone number: _____ Cell phone number: _____

E-mail address: _____

Coach: _____

Phone number: _____ Cell phone number: _____

E-mail address: _____

OTHER AFTER-SCHOOL ACTIVITY: _____

Name of child: _____

Day of activity: _____

Time: _____

Location: _____

Teacher: _____

Phone number: _____ Cell phone number: _____

E-mail address: _____

OTHER AFTER-SCHOOL ACTIVITY: _____

Name of child: _____

Day of activity: _____

Time: _____

Location: _____

Teacher: _____

Phone number: _____ Cell phone number: _____

E-mail address: _____

OTHER AFTER-SCHOOL ACTIVITY: _____

Name of child: _____

Day of activity: _____

Time: _____

Location: _____

Teacher: _____

Phone number: _____ Cell phone number: _____

E-mail address: _____

CAMP CONTACT INFORMATION

NAME OF CHILD: _____

Camp name: _____

    Phone number: _____ Camp e-mail address: _____

    Address: _____

Director: _____

    Phone number: _____ Cell phone number: _____

    E-mail address: _____

Group name/number: _____

Counselor: _____

    Phone number: _____ Cell phone number: _____

Counselor: _____

    Phone number: _____ Cell phone number: _____

Bus number: _____ Bus driver: _____

Bus monitor: _____

    Cell phone number: _____

NAME OF CHILD: _____

Camp name: _____

    Phone number: _____ Camp e-mail address: _____

    Address: _____

Director: _____

    Phone number: _____ Cell phone number: _____

    E-mail address: _____

Group name/number: _____

Counselor: _____

    Phone number: _____ Cell phone number: _____

Counselor: _____

    Phone number: _____ Cell phone number: _____

Bus number: _____ Bus driver: _____

Bus monitor: _____

    Cell phone number: _____

NAME OF CHILD: _____

  Camp name: _____

    Phone number: _____ Camp e-mail address: _____

    Address: _____

  Director: _____

    Phone number: _____ Cell phone number: _____

    E-mail address: _____

  Group name/number: _____

  Counselor: _____

    Phone number: _____ Cell phone number: _____

  Counselor: _____

    Phone number: _____ Cell phone number: _____

  Bus number: _____ Bus driver: _____

  Bus monitor: _____

    Cell phone number: _____

SUNSCREEN SMARTS

Whether your child is at camp, you're in the garden, or your family is walking to the library, you all need sunscreen and lip protectant. Follow these five steps to banish sunburn from summer:

➤ Apply sunscreen 15 to 30 minutes before you venture outside.

➤ Use a sunscreen that has an SPF of at least 30. Pick one that also offers "broad spectrum" coverage.

➤ Reapply sunscreen every two hours—or more often if you've been in the water or sweating a lot.

➤ Make sure you use enough sunscreen. Envision a shotglass full of sunscreen; that's the right amount for full coverage.

➤ Don't be fooled into thinking that a shirt will protect you from sunburn. A white t-shirt, for example, may have an SPF of less than five.

CARPOOL LISTS

REASON FOR CARPOOL: _____

From where to where: _____

My day to drive: _____

Name of other driver: _____

    Day to drive: _____

    Phone number: _____ Cell phone number: _____

    E-mail address: _____

    Name of child: _____

Name of other driver: _____

    Day to drive: _____

    Phone number: _____ Cell phone number: _____

    E-mail address: _____

    Name of child: _____

Name of other driver: _____

    Day to drive: _____

    Phone number: _____ Cell phone number: _____

    E-mail address: _____

    Name of child: _____

REASON FOR CARPOOL: _____

From where to where: _____

My day to drive: _____

Name of other driver: _____

    Day to drive: _____

    Phone number: _____ Cell phone number: _____

    E-mail address: _____

    Name of child: _____

Name of other driver: _____

    Day to drive: _____

    Phone number: _____ Cell phone number: _____

E-mail address: _____

Name of child: _____

Name of other driver: _____

    Day to drive: _____

    Phone number: _____ Cell phone number: _____

    E-mail address: _____

    Name of child: _____

REASON FOR CARPOOL: _____

From where to where: _____

My day to drive: _____

Name of other driver: _____

    Day to drive: _____

    Phone number: _____ Cell phone number: _____

    E-mail address: _____

    Name of child: _____

Name of other driver: _____

    Day to drive: _____

    Phone number: _____ Cell phone number: _____

    E-mail address: _____

    Name of child: _____

Name of other driver: _____

    Day to drive: _____

    Phone number: _____ Cell phone number: _____

    E-mail address: _____

    Name of child: _____

SCHOOL DATES TO REMEMBER

Use the calendar below to record dates of parent-teacher conferences, standardized tests, field trips, fundraisers, school vacations, concerts and plays, picture-taking days, the first and last days of school, and any other school-related information that you don't want to forget.

SEPTEMBER _____

_____

_____

_____

_____

_____

_____

_____

OCTOBER _____

_____

_____

_____

_____

_____

_____

_____

NOVEMBER _____

_____

_____

_____

_____

_____

_____

DECEMBER _____

_____
_____
_____
_____
_____
_____
_____

JANUARY _____

_____
_____
_____
_____
_____
_____
_____

FEBRUARY _____

_____
_____
_____
_____
_____
_____
_____

MARCH _____

_____
_____
_____

APRIL _____

MAY _____

JUNE _____

SCHOOL SUPPLIES

Although many teachers specify the school supplies they expect each child to bring at the beginning of the school year, they generally ask parents to send in a substantial number of the following items. It's also a good idea to have some of these supplies on hand at home for homework and in case your child runs out of an item in the middle of the year. This list covers K-12, so some of the items may not apply to your child's particular year of school.

- ☐ Binder(s)
- ☐ Backpack
- ☐ Calculator
- ☐ Colored pencils
- ☐ Composition books
- ☐ Crayons
- ☐ Erasers
- ☐ Folders
- ☐ Glue or glue stick
- ☐ Highlighters
- ☐ Hole reinforcements
- ☐ Index cards
- ☐ Liquid correction fluid
- ☐ Loose-leaf paper

- ☐ Lunch box
- ☐ Markers
- ☐ Pencil case
- ☐ Pencil sharpener
- ☐ Pencils
- ☐ Pens
- ☐ Post-it notes
- ☐ Ruler
- ☐ Scissors
- ☐ Spiral notebooks
- ☐ Subject dividers (for binder)
- ☐ Tissues
- ☐ 3-hole ring punch

PAPER AND PENS TIMES TEN

Save money on school supplies by buying pencils, pens, tape, and notebooks in bulk at an office-supply store. You'll save a bundle and won't have to run out to buy another item every time your child remembers at the last minute that he needs something for school.

Grooming and Family Attire

CONTACT INFORMATION

BARBER: _____

    Phone number: _____

    Address: _____

COLORIST: _____

    Phone number: _____

    Address: _____

HAIRDRESSER (FOR ADULTS): _____

    Phone number: _____

    Address: _____

HAIRDRESSER (FOR CHILDREN): _____

    Phone number: _____

    Address: _____

MANICURIST: _____

    Phone number: _____

    Address: _____

OTHER PERSONAL CARE PROFESSIONAL: _____

    Phone number: _____

    Address: _____

OTHER PERSONAL CARE PROFESSIONAL: _____

    Phone number: _____

    Address: _____

CLOTHING SIZES

NAME (FEMALE): _____

Bathing suit: _____   Dress: _____

Belt: _____   Dress pants: _____

Blazer: _____   Jeans: _____

Coat/jacket: _____   Pajamas: _____

Shirt/blouse: _____ Stockings/tights: _____

Shoes/boots: _____ Sweater: _____

Shorts: _____ Underwear: _____

Skirt: _____ Other: _____

Socks: _____ Other: _____

NAME (FEMALE): _____

Bathing suit: _____ Shoes/boots: _____

Belt: _____ Shorts: _____

Blazer: _____ Skirt: _____

Coat/jacket: _____ Socks: _____

Dress: _____ Stockings/tights: _____

Dress pants: _____ Sweater: _____

Jeans: _____ Underwear: _____

Pajamas: _____ Other: _____

Shirt/blouse: _____ Other: _____

NAME (FEMALE): _____

Bathing suit: _____ Shoes/boots: _____

Belt: _____ Shorts: _____

Blazer: _____ Skirt: _____

Coat/jacket: _____ Socks: _____

Dress: _____ Stockings/tights: _____

Dress pants: _____ Sweater: _____

Jeans: _____ Underwear: _____

Pajamas: _____ Other: _____

Shirt/blouse: _____ Other: _____

NAME (MALE): _____

Belt: _____ Dress shirt: _____

Coat/jacket: _____ Jeans: _____

Dress pants: _____ Pajamas: _____

Shoes/boots : _____

Shorts: _____

Socks: _____

Sport coat: _____

Sport shirt: _____

Suit: _____

    Jacket: _____

Pants: _____

Sweater: _____

Swim trunks: _____

Underwear: _____

Other: _____

Other: _____

Other: _____

NAME (MALE): _____

Belt: _____

Coat/jacket: _____

Dress pants: _____

Dress shirt: _____

Jeans: _____

Pajamas: _____

Shoes/boots : _____

Shorts: _____

Socks: _____

Sport coat: _____

Sport shirt: _____

Suit: _____

    Jacket: _____

    Pants: _____

Sweater: _____

Swim trunks: _____

Underwear: _____

Other: _____

Other: _____

Other: _____

NAME (MALE): _____

Belt: _____

Coat/jacket: _____

Dress pants: _____

Dress shirt: _____

Jeans: _____

Pajamas: _____

Shoes/boots : _____

Shorts: _____

Socks: _____

Sport coat: _____

Sport shirt: _____

Suit: _____

    Jacket: _____

    Pants: _____

Sweater: _____

Swim trunks: _____

Underwear: _____

Other: _____

Other: _____

Other: _____

WHOLESALE SHOPPING

WHOLESALE CLUB: _____

    Phone number: _____

    Address: _____

    Membership number: _____ Expiration date: _____

SUBSCRIPTIONS

NEWSPAPER: _____

    Customer service phone number: _____

    Date of renewal: _____ Cost: _____

NEWSPAPER: _____

    Customer service phone number: _____

    Date of renewal: _____ Cost: _____

MAGAZINE: _____

    Customer service phone number: _____

    Date of renewal: _____ Cost: _____

MAGAZINE: _____

    Customer service phone number: _____

    Date of renewal: _____ Cost: _____

MAGAZINE: _____

    Customer service phone number: _____

    Date of renewal: _____ Cost: _____

MAGAZINE: _____

    Customer service phone number: _____

    Date of renewal: _____ Cost: _____

Pets

VITAL STATISTICS

NAME OF PET: _____

   Date of birth: _____

NAME OF PET: _____

   Date of birth: _____

CONTACT INFORMATION

BREEDER: _____

   Phone number: _____ Cell phone number: _____

   Fax number: _____ E-mail address: _____

   Address: _____

DOG WALKER: _____

   Phone number: _____ Cell phone number: _____

   Fax number: _____ E-mail address: _____

   Address: _____

FENCE COMPANY: _____

   Phone number: _____ Cell phone number: _____

   Fax number: _____ E-mail address: _____

   Address: _____

GROOMER: _____

   Phone number: _____ Cell phone number: _____

   Fax number: _____ E-mail address: _____

   Address: _____

KENNEL: _____

   Phone number: _____ Cell phone number: _____

   Fax number: _____ E-mail address: _____

   Address: _____

OBEDIENCE SCHOOL: _____

   Phone number: _____ Cell phone number: _____

Fax number: _____ E-mail address: _____

Address: _____

PET INSURANCE AGENCY: _____

    Agent: _____

    Phone number: _____ Cell phone number: _____

    Fax number: _____ E-mail address: _____

    Address: _____

PET SITTER: _____

    Phone number: _____ Cell phone number: _____

    Fax number: _____ E-mail address: _____

    Address: _____

PET STORE: _____

    Phone number: _____

    Fax number: _____ E-mail address: _____

    Address: _____

PET SUPPLY CATALOG: _____

    Phone number: _____

    Fax number: _____ E-mail address: _____

    Address: _____

VETERINARIAN: _____

    Phone number: _____ Cell phone number: _____

    Emergency phone number: _____

    Fax number: _____ E-mail address: _____

    Address: _____

PREPARING FOR A PUPPY

Help new dog owners welcome home their puppy with a pet first-aid kit. Fill a basket with these essential first-aid items that all dog owners should have on hand:

- ➤ Antibiotic ointment
- ➤ Baby thermometer
- ➤ Benadryl (to help stop insect bites from itching)
- ➤ Cotton balls
- ➤ Ear-cleaning solution
- ➤ Gauze
- ➤ Hydrocortisone spray or ointment
- ➤ Mild dog shampoo
- ➤ Nail clippers for dogs
- ➤ Oral medication syringes
- ➤ Saline eyewash
- ➤ Tweezers (for removing ticks)

Other veterinarians in the practice: _____

_____

HEALTH

ANNUAL CHECKUP (WITH IMMUNIZATIONS)

Date: _____

Veterinarian: _____

MEDICINE: _____

Quantity: _____

Date/time administered: _____

_____

_____

MEDICINE: _____

Quantity: _____

Date/time administered: _____

_____

_____

MEDICINE: _____

Quantity: _____

Date/time administered: _____

_____

_____

MEDICINE: _____

Quantity: _____

Date/time administered: _____

_____

_____

VITAMINS: _____

Quantity: _____

Date/time administered: _____

_____

VITAMINS: _____

   Quantity: _____

   Date/time administered: _____

_____

_____

SAFETY

DATE TO REPLACE BATTERIES IN COLLAR (FOR INVISIBLE FENCE): _____

CODE NUMBER FOR PET TRACKING DEVICE: _____

Notes

trevorcole-art.com   —artist

tricia hodgins.com   — artist

imgi.ca   —herbalife

weightlossite.com   —herbalife

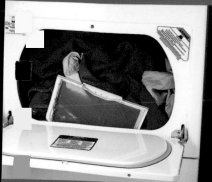

Cleaning
and Clothing
Care

Cleaning and Clothing Care

In the pages that follow you'll find space to write in the names, phone numbers, and addresses of the services you use to keep your house and clothes spotless, like carpet cleaners and dry cleaners; a list of supplies you'll need as you tackle your chores; suggestions for daily, weekly, and spring cleaning; helpful tips for housecleaning and clothing care; and a guide that helps you decipher fabric-care symbols. Don't forget to save garment care labels, dry cleaning receipts, and business cards in the pocket provided.

Clean House, Clean Clothes

CONTACT INFORMATION

AREA RUG CLEANING COMPANY: _____

    Phone number: _____ Fax number: _____

    Address: _____

    E-mail address: _____

    Date of service: _____ Cost: _____

CARPET CLEANING COMPANY: _____

    Phone number: _____ Fax number: _____

    Address: _____

    E-mail address: _____

    Date of service: _____ Cost: _____

CLEANING SERVICE/HOUSEKEEPER: _____

    Phone number: _____ Fax number: _____

    Address: _____

    E-mail address: _____

    Date of service: _____ Cost: _____

CURTAIN/DRAPERY CLEANING SERVICE: _____

    Phone number: _____ Fax number: _____

    Address: _____

    E-mail address: _____

    Date of service: _____ Cost: _____

DRY CLEANER: _____

    Phone number: _____ Fax number: _____

    Address: _____

    E-mail address: _____

    Date of service: _____ Cost: _____

UPHOLSTERY CLEANING SERVICE: _____

    Phone number: _____ Fax number: _____

    Address: _____

    E-mail address: _____

    Date of service: _____ Cost: _____

WINDOW CLEANING SERVICE: _____

    Phone number: _____ Fax number: _____

    Address: _____

    E-mail address: _____

    Date of service: _____ Cost: _____

OTHER: _____

    Phone number: _____ Fax number: _____

    Address: _____

    E-mail address: _____

    Date of service: _____ Cost: _____

OTHER:

    Phone number: _____ Fax number: _____

    Address: _____

    E-mail address: _____

    Date of service: _____ Cost: _____

CLEAN UP CALENDAR

Most people hate to clean house. In these busy times, it makes sense to be flexible and do only what you need to do so you can make the most of your leisure time. This timetable suggests tasks that can help you stay on top of the job.

	KITCHEN	BATHROOM	AROUND THE HOUSE
DAILY	• Dispose of trash and recyclables	• Wipe fixtures, chrome, and counter-tops	• Put clothing, books, toys, and other items where they belong
	• Hand wash and dry dishes or place them in the dishwasher (machine wash when a full load has accumulated)	• Straighten towels	• Straighten living spaces and bedrooms
	• Wipe table, counter-tops, and range top	• Use a squeegee or daily shower cleaner to prevent streaks and soap scum buildup	• Make beds
	• Wash coffeemaker after each use		• Go through the mail; handle or recycle, as needed
	• Run food disposal and clean the sink		
	• Sweep or vacuum floor; wipe up any spots with a damp paper towel		

VACUUM BAG AND FILTER FACTS

Change your vacuum bag when it's two–thirds full in order to keep the suction strong. If you have a bagless vacuum, clean out the dirt container after you've used it twice.

Once a month, remove the filter from the dust cup of your bagless vacuum and either tap it clean or rinse it. Check filters on all other vacuums once every six months.

	KITCHEN	BATHROOM	AROUND THE HOUSE
WEEKLY	• Thoroughly clean range top and front, drip pans, control knobs, and backsplash	• Scrub bathtubs and sinks	• Dust furniture, books, pictures, lamp bases and shades, and electronics
	• Wipe microwave oven, both inside and outside	• Clean mirrors	• Vacuum floors and upholstery—and woodwork, as needed
	• Organize refrigerator and wipe spills; dispose of spoiled leftover foods	• Clean shower stalls and doors and disinfect toilets	• Wipe smudges off walls and woodwork
	• Clean items on countertop; move them away from walls to wipe under and behind	• Clean toothbrush and soap holders	• Empty wastepaper baskets
	• Sweep or vacuum and wash floor	• Wipe tile surfaces	• Change bed linens
	• Wipe table and chairs	• Vacuum and wash floors	• Clean the mirrors, if needed
			• Recycle or toss newspapers older than a week and magazines older than 3 months

CLEANING CHECKLIST

How—and even when—you embark on a "spring cleaning" depends on your schedule, your standards, and your priorities. The following checklist notes all the tasks to make your house sparkle; you may choose to do them all, or only those you feel are most important.

THE KITCHEN

☐ Wipe the outside of the refrigerator

☐ Clean the top of the refrigerator

☐ Vacuum refrigerator coils

☐ Clean the inside of the refrigerator (bins, shelves, and walls)

☐ Clean under the refrigerator

☐ Wipe the outside of kitchen cabinets

☐ Clean the insides of kitchen cabinets and drawers

☐ Degrime the exhaust fan and hood

☐ Clean the oven

☐ Wash the kitchen floor

THE BATHROOM

☐ Replace the shower curtain liner

☐ Scrub tub grout

☐ Thoroughly clean shower doors

☐ Clean out the medicine cabinet

☐ Scrub behind the toilet

☐ Wash the bathroom floor

GENERAL TASKS

☐ Wipe down walls, light switches, and doorknobs

☐ Use vacuum attachments to clean baseboards, heating vents, windowsills, and tops of bookcases

☐ Wash baseboards

☐ Use vacuum dusting brush tool to clean lampshades

☐ Move furniture and then vacuum underneath

☐ Shampoo carpets and launder washable throw rugs

☐ Clean and/or polish wood floors

☐ Clean light fixtures

- ☐ Dust tops of mirrors and picture frames
- ☐ Clean mirrors
- ☐ Throw away outdated newspapers and magazines
- ☐ Dust all surfaces
- ☐ Polish chrome fixtures
- ☐ Wash all windows
- ☐ Wash window blinds
- ☐ Launder curtains
- ☐ Clean blades on ceiling fans and blades and grills on window fans
- ☐ Clean or replace air-conditioning filters
- ☐ Vacuum fireplace ashes; clean fireplace, fireplace fixtures, and fireplace tools
- ☐ Wash painted walls and ceilings
- ☐ Clean linen closet; refold linens and toss worn or stained linens
- ☐ Clean humidifiers and dehumidifiers when in use

FURNITURE

- ☐ Remove books from shelves and dust bookcases
- ☐ Clean contents of china cabinet; dust and clean china cabinet's glass and mirrors
- ☐ Polish furniture
- ☐ Spot-clean upholstery
- ☐ Fluff up decorative pillows
- ☐ Clean piano keys
- ☐ Clean computer equipment
- ☐ Clean stereo equipment
- ☐ Eliminate clutter beneath beds, then vacuum
- ☐ Wash bedding, including mattress pads and blankets
- ☐ Vacuum mattress

CRACK THE CODE

Not sure how to clean your upholstery? To solve the mystery, look for these codes on the piece of furniture in question or on a sample piece of fabric:

W Use a water-based product—foam from a mild detergent works well—or a nonsolvent upholstery shampoo

S Use a solvent-based cleaner to clean the fabric

WS Use either a nonsolvent cleaner or a solvent-based cleaner

X Get the fabric cleaned by a professional

CLEANING SHOPPING LIST

SPECIFIC LIST

Record here the particular types/brands/sizes you need for your cleaning tools.

Mop head: _____

Vacuum cleaner bags: _____ _____

Vacuum filter: _____

GENERAL LIST

This list will help you keep the cleaning supplies you need on hand for spring cleaning and everyday cleaning. (It also assumes you already have the cleaning tools you need—a vacuum cleaner, a wet mop, a dry mop, a scrub brush, and so on.) Note your favorite products next to the supplies: You'll find shopping easier when you know exactly what you want.

☐ Abrasive cleanser

☐ Air/fabric/carpet/room freshener, deodorizer, odor eliminators

☐ All-purpose cleaner

☐ Ammonia

☐ Baking soda

☐ Brass polish

☐ Carpet cleaners (including spot cleaners)

☐ Dishwashing detergent for sink

☐ Dishwasher detergent

☐ Drain cleaners

☐ Dusting spray

☐ Furniture polish

☐ Glass cleaner

☐ Mildew remover

☐ Oven cleaner

☐ Sanitizing/disinfecting wipes

☐ Scouring pads

☐ Silver polish

☐ Toilet bowl cleaner

☐ Tub, tile, and sink cleaner

☐ Upholstery cleaner

☐ Vinegar

☐ Wood floor cleaner

TOOLS OF THE TRADE

Keeping cleaning tools on hand is just as important as stocking up on cleaning supplies. Don't forget to keep these tools together and ready to use:

Bucket	Scrub brush
Dry mop	Sponges
Dust cloths	Stepstool/stepladder
(including electrostatic dust cloths)	Toilet bowl brush
Gloves	Vacuum
Paper towels	Wet mop

CLOTHING CARE SHOPPING LIST
Here are the products you need to keep near your washer and dryer. Again, you may choose to note your favorite brands to keep shopping simpler.

- ☐ Chlorine bleach and non-chlorine bleach
- ☐ Detergent for fine washables
- ☐ Dryer sheets
- ☐ Fabric softener
- ☐ Laundry detergent
- ☐ Spray starch
- ☐ Stain removers

BUTTON BOX

Don't throw away the little envelopes that hold extra buttons for your new clothes. Instead, label the envelopes with specific details about the clothes they belong to—light blue and white patterned blouse, for example—and save them in a pretty box. When you need to replace a button, you'll know exactly where to find it.

PREPARE YOUR SHOES FOR THE SUMMER

Ask a shoe repair professional to clean the insole sock lining (the leather base that holds your foot). Cleaning and repairing this part of your sandal or other summer-style shoe gives it a complete makeover. Don't forget to replace worn heels as well, and remember that replacing worn soles will extend the life of your shoes.

LABEL LANGUAGE

The care symbols on your clothes often seem incomprehensible. This guide will help you determine at a glance exactly how to care for your entire wardrobe. You may want to photocopy this chart and hang it near your washing machine.

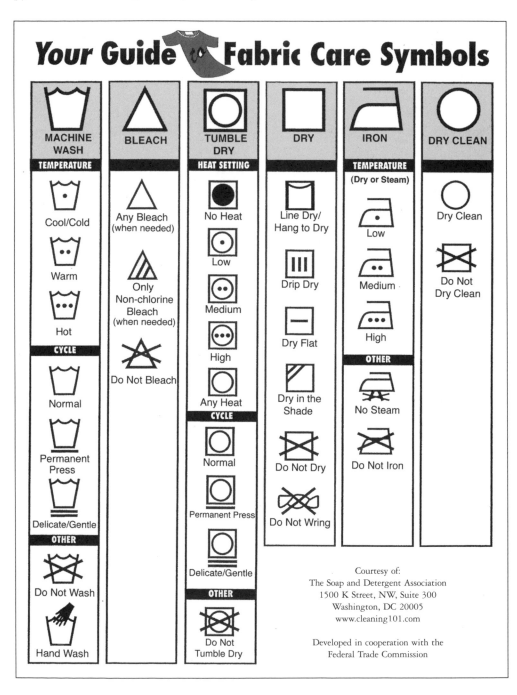

Your Guide to Fabric Care Symbols

MACHINE WASH	BLEACH	TUMBLE DRY	DRY	IRON	DRY CLEAN

Courtesy of:
The Soap and Detergent Association
1500 K Street, NW, Suite 300
Washington, DC 20005
www.cleaning101.com

Developed in cooperation with the
Federal Trade Commission

Notes

Notes

Decorating

Decorating

Whether you love choosing paint colors and tiles for your new bathroom or can't bear the thought of deciding which window treatment will look best in your living room, this section will serve your decorating needs. This is where you'll record the names, phone numbers, and other contact information for the people who help you decorate your home; the measurements for floors, walls, and windows in each room of your house; and details about the colors and fabrics you've chosen for each room. You can even jot down information about smaller decorating details—the size and shape of your tablecloth, the type, size, and wattage of light bulbs you need (in the "Furniture and Fixtures" tables), and your china pattern, for example—so you never have to hunt through your house for that information again. And don't forget to keep in the pocket paint chips, fabric swatches, business cards, and important receipts.

Your Indoor Living Space

CONTACT INFORMATION

ARCHITECT: _____

    Phone number: _____ Cell phone number: _____

    Fax number: _____ E-mail address: _____

    Address: _____

CARPENTER: _____

    Phone number: _____ Cell phone number: _____

    Fax number: _____ E-mail address: _____

    Address: _____

CONTRACTOR: _____

    Phone number: _____ Cell phone number: _____

    Fax number: _____ E-mail address: _____

    Address: _____

HANDYMAN: _____

    Phone number: _____ Cell phone number: _____

    Fax number: _____ E-mail address: _____

    Address: _____

HOME CENTER: _____

    Phone number: _____

    Fax number: _____ E-mail address: _____

    Address: _____

INSTALLATION (FLOOR)

    Phone number: _____ Cell phone number: _____

    Fax number: _____ E-mail address: _____

    Address: _____

INSTALLATION (WINDOW TREATMENTS)

    Phone number: _____ Cell phone number: _____

    Fax number: _____ E-mail address: _____

    Address: _____

INTERIOR DECORATOR: _____

    Phone number: _____ Cell phone number: _____

    Fax number: _____ E-mail address: _____

    Address: _____

PAINTER (INTERIOR): _____

    Phone number: _____ Cell phone number: _____

    Fax number: _____ E-mail address: _____

    Address: _____

PICTURE FRAMER: _____

    Phone number: _____ Cell phone number: _____

    Fax number: _____ E-mail address: _____

    Address: _____

REFINISHER: _____

    Phone number: _____ Cell phone number: _____

    Fax number: _____ E-mail address: _____

    Address: _____

WALLPAPER REMOVER/HANGER: _____

    Phone number: _____ Cell phone number: _____

    Fax number: _____ E-mail address: _____

    Address: _____

OTHER: _____

    Phone number: _____ Cell phone number: _____

    Fax number: _____ E-mail address: _____

    Address: _____

OTHER: _____

    Phone number: _____ Cell phone number: _____

    Fax number: _____ E-mail address: _____

    Address: _____

OTHER: _____

    Phone number: _____ Cell phone number: _____

    Fax number: _____ E-mail address: _____

    Address: _____

DECORATING DETAILS

Use the following spaces to record all the details you need to remember about how you have decorated your home. This information will be invaluable the next time you repaint your walls, change your window treatments, or refinish your floor.

LIVING ROOM

FLOOR COVERING

Floor measurements: _____

Type of floor: _____

    Brand: _____

    Color: _____ Pattern: _____

Type of backing: _____

Purchased from: _____ Date: _____ Cost: _____

Date installed: _____

WINDOW TREATMENTS

Window location: _____

    Measurements

        Height: _____ Width: _____

        Top of window to floor: _____

    Type of treatment: _____

        Height: _____ Width: _____

        Purchased from: _____ Date: _____ Cost: _____

        Date installed: _____

Window location: _____

    Measurements

        Height: _____ Width: _____

        Top of window to floor: _____

    Type of treatment: _____

        Height: _____ Width: _____

        Purchased from: _____ Date: _____ Cost: _____

        Date installed: _____

WALL COVERING

Wall measurements

    North: _____ South: _____

    East: _____ West: _____

Brand: _____

Pattern: _____

Color and number: _____

Purchased from: _____ Date: _____ Cost: _____

Date installed: _____

ITEM	PURCHASED FROM	DATE	COST	COMMENTS
LIVING ROOM FURNITURE AND FIXTURES				

MAKE YOUR OWN FURNITURE

Turn a stack of books that have already been read into a practical side table. Put the heaviest books on the floor, add smaller books in the middle, and place a large book on the top as the tabletop. Use Fun-Tak between the books to keep them from sliding off one another.

DINING ROOM

FLOOR COVERING

Floor measurements: _____

Type of floor: _____

    Brand: _____

    Color: _____ Pattern: _____

Type of backing: _____

Purchased from: _____ Date: _____ Cost:_____

Date installed: _____

WINDOW TREATMENTS

Window location: _____

    Measurements

        Height: _____ Width: _____

        Top of window to floor: _____

    Type of treatment: _____

        Height: _____ Width: _____

        Purchased from: _____ Date: _____ Cost:_____

        Date installed: _____

Window location: _____

    Measurements

        Height: _____ Width: _____

        Top of window to floor: _____

    Type of treatment: _____

        Height: _____ Width: _____

        Purchased from: _____ Date: _____ Cost:_____

        Date installed: _____

WALL COVERING

Wall measurements

    North: _____ South: _____

    East: _____ West: _____

Brand: _____

Pattern: _____

Color and number: _____

Purchased from: _____ Date: _____ Cost: _____

Date installed: _____

HANG ON!

If you decide to hang your own wallpaper, be sure not to press hard on the seams. If you do, you'll push the glue away from the seams, leaving them more likely to peel at a later date.

ITEM	PURCHASED FROM	DATE	COST	COMMENTS
DINING ROOM FURNITURE AND FIXTURES				

TABLECLOTH

Table with leaves

Shape: _____ Size: _____

Table without leaves

Shape: _____ Size: _____

CHINA PATTERN: _____

SILVER PATTERN: _____

FLATWARE PATTERN: _____

DINING ROOM DÉCOR

Spruce up your dining room by covering dining-room chair seats with fabric remnants. Use different patterns for a striking visual effect.

KITCHEN

Floor covering

Floor measurements: _____

Type of floor: _____

    Brand: _____

    Color: _____ Pattern: _____

Type of backing: _____

    Purchased from: _____ Date: _____ Cost:_____

    Date installed: _____

Window treatments

Window location: _____

    Measurements

        Height: _____ Width: _____

        Top of window to floor: _____

    Type of treatment: _____

        Height: _____ Width: _____

        Purchased from: _____ Date: _____ Cost:_____

        Date installed: _____

Window location: _____

    Measurements

        Height: _____ Width: _____

        Top of window to floor: _____

    Type of treatment: _____

        Height: _____ Width: _____

        Purchased from: _____ Date: _____ Cost:_____

        Date installed: _____

Wall covering

Wall measurements

    North: _____ South: _____

    East: _____ West: _____

Brand: _____

Pattern: _____

Color and number: _____

Purchased from: _____ Date: _____ Cost: _____

Date installed: _____

KITCHEN FURNITURE AND FIXTURES				
ITEM	PURCHASED FROM	DATE	COST	COMMENTS

CABINETS

Brand: _____

Style: _____

Material: _____

Stain/paint color and number: _____

Purchased from: _____ Date: _____ Cost: _____

Date installed: _____

COUNTERTOP

Brand: _____

Material: _____

Purchased from: _____ Date: _____ Cost: _____

Date installed: _____

BEDROOM #1

FLOOR COVERING

Floor measurements: _____

Type of floor: _____

    Brand: _____

    Color: _____ Pattern: _____

Type of backing: _____

      Purchased from: _____ Date: _____ Cost:_____

Date installed: _____

WINDOW TREATMENTS

Window location: _____

    Measurements

      Height: _____ Width: _____

      Top of window to floor: _____

    Type of treatment: _____

      Height: _____Width: _____

      Purchased from: _____ Date: _____ Cost:_____

      Date installed: _____

Window location: _____

    Measurements

      Height: _____ Width: _____

      Top of window to floor: _____

    Type of treatment: _____

      Height: _____Width: _____

      Purchased from: _____ Date: _____ Cost:_____

      Date installed: _____

WALL COVERING

Wall measurements

    North: _____ South: _____

    East: _____ West: _____

Brand: _____

Pattern: _____

Color and number: _____

Purchased from: _____ Date: _____ Cost:_____

Date installed: _____

BEDROOM #1 FURNITURE AND FIXTURES				
ITEM	PURCHASED FROM	DATE	COST	COMMENTS

BEDROOM #2

FLOOR COVERING

Floor measurements: _____

Type of floor: _____

    Brand: _____

    Color: _____ Pattern: _____

Type of backing: _____

Purchased from: _____ Date: _____ Cost:_____

Date installed: _____

WINDOW TREATMENTS

Window location: _____

    Measurements

      Height: _____ Width: _____

      Top of window to floor: _____

      Type of treatment: _____

Height: _____ Width: _____

Purchased from: _____ Date: _____ Cost: _____

Date installed: _____

Window location: _____

Measurements

Height: _____ Width: _____

Top of window to floor: _____

Type of treatment: _____

Height: _____ Width: _____

Purchased from: _____ Date: _____ Cost: _____

Date installed: _____

WALL COVERING

Wall measurements

North: _____ South: _____

East: _____ West: _____

Brand: _____

Pattern: _____

Color and number: _____

Purchased from: _____ Date: _____ Cost: _____

Date installed: _____

BEDROOM #2 FURNITURE AND FIXTURES				
ITEM	PURCHASED FROM	DATE	COST	COMMENTS

BEDROOM #3

FLOOR COVERING

Floor measurements: _____

Type of floor: _____

    Brand: _____

    Color: _____ Pattern: _____

Type of backing: _____

Purchased from: _____ Date: _____ Cost:_____

Date installed: _____

WINDOW TREATMENTS

Window location: _____

    Measurements

      Height: _____ Width: _____

      Top of window to floor: _____

    Type of treatment: _____

      Height: _____ Width: _____

      Purchased from: _____ Date: _____ Cost:_____

      Date installed: _____

Window location: _____

    Measurements

    Height: _____ Width: _____

      Top of window to floor: _____

    Type of treatment: _____

    Height: _____ Width: _____

      Purchased from: _____ Date: _____ Cost:_____

      Date installed: _____

WALL COVERING

Wall measurements

    North: _____ South: _____

    East: _____ West: _____

Brand: _____

Pattern: _____

Color and number: _____

Purchased from: _____ Date: _____ Cost: _____

Date installed: _____

BEDROOM #3 FURNITURE AND FIXTURES				
ITEM	PURCHASED FROM	DATE	COST	COMMENTS

BEDROOM #4

FLOOR COVERING

Floor measurements: _____

Type of floor: _____

    Brand: _____

    Color: _____ Pattern: _____

Type of backing: _____

Purchased from: _____ Date: _____ Cost:_____

Date installed: _____

WINDOW TREATMENTS

Window location: _____

    Measurements

      Height: _____ Width: _____

      Top of window to floor: _____

    Type of treatment: _____

Height: _____ Width: _____

Purchased from: _____ Date: _____ Cost: _____

Date installed: _____

Window location: _____

   Measurements

     Height: _____ Width: _____

     Top of window to floor: _____

   Type of treatment: _____

     Height: _____ Width: _____

     Purchased from: _____ Date: _____ Cost: _____

     Date installed: _____

WALL COVERING

Wall measurements

   North: _____ South: _____

   East: _____ West: _____

Brand: _____

Pattern: _____

Color and number: _____

Purchased from: _____ Date: _____ Cost: _____

Date installed: _____

BEDROOM #4 FURNITURE AND FIXTURES				
ITEM	PURCHASED FROM	DATE	COST	COMMENTS

PERFECT PAINTING

Painting furniture is easy, but you still need to follow a few simple rules to get the best results. Here's what you need to know:

➤ Always prepare the surface. Repair what needs repairing, then clean the furniture with water and a mild soap (like dish detergent). Finish preparing it by sanding off any old varnish.

➤ Protect the piece's glass and hardware. Line any windows with low-tack tape and cover the hinges, handles, and knobs you don't want to paint.

➤ Start with a coat of primer. It will help the paint stick to the piece and hide imperfections like knots. Let the primer dry for about two hours before you continue.

➤ Paint a base coat. Use a semi- or high-gloss interior latex paint (paints with a high sheen are easier to clean). Let the base dry for an hour, then apply a second coat.

➤ Add accent colors or simple shapes like diamonds. Make straight lines on design elements by bordering the shapes with tape, then painting them.

BATHROOM #1

FLOOR COVERING

Floor measurements: _____

Type of floor: _____

    Brand: _____

    Color: _____ Pattern: _____

Type of backing: _____

Purchased from: _____ Date: _____ Cost: _____

Date installed: _____

WINDOW TREATMENTS

Window location: _____

    Measurements

      Height: _____ Width: _____

      Top of window to floor: _____

    Type of treatment: _____

      Height: _____ Width: _____

      Purchased from: _____ Date: _____ Cost: _____

      Date installed: _____

WALL COVERING

Wall measurements

North: _____ South: _____

East: _____ West: _____

Brand: _____

Pattern: _____

Color and number: _____

Purchased from: _____ Date: _____ Cost: _____

Date installed: _____

BATHROOM #1 FURNITURE AND FIXTURES				
ITEM	PURCHASED FROM	DATE	COST	COMMENTS

BATHROOM #2

FLOOR COVERING

Floor measurements: _____

Type of floor: _____

Brand: _____

Color: _____ Pattern: _____

Type of backing: _____

Purchased from: _____ Date: _____ Cost: _____

Date installed: _____

WINDOW TREATMENTS

Window location: _____

    Measurements

      Height: _____ Width: _____

      Top of window to floor: _____

    Type of treatment: _____

      Height: _____Width: _____

      Purchased from: _____ Date: _____ Cost:_____

      Date installed: _____

WALL COVERING

Wall measurements

    North: _____South: _____

    East: _____ West: _____

Brand: _____

Pattern: _____

Color and number: _____

Purchased from: _____ Date: _____Cost: _____

Date installed: _____

BATHROOM #2 FURNITURE AND FIXTURES				
ITEM	PURCHASED FROM	DATE	COST	COMMENTS

A CEILING TRICK

Want to make your room look bigger? Paint the ceiling either sky blue or lavender.

BATHROOM #3

FLOOR COVERING

Floor measurements: _____

Type of floor: _____

    Brand: _____

    Color: _____ Pattern: _____

Type of backing: _____

Purchased from: _____ Date: _____Cost: _____

Date installed: _____

WINDOW TREATMENTS

Window location: _____

    Measurements

        Height: _____ Width: _____

        Top of window to floor: _____

    Type of treatment: _____

        Height: _____Width: _____

        Purchased from: _____ Date: _____ Cost:_____

        Date installed: _____

WALL COVERING

Wall measurements

    North: _____South: _____

    East: _____ West: _____

Brand: _____

Pattern: _____

Color and number: _____

Purchased from: _____ Date: _____Cost: _____

Date installed: _____

BATHROOM #3 FURNITURE AND FIXTURES

ITEM	PURCHASED FROM	DATE	COST	COMMENTS

OFFICE

FLOOR COVERING

Floor measurements: _____

Type of floor: _____

    Brand: _____

    Color: _____ Pattern: _____

Type of backing: _____

Purchased from: _____ Date: _____ Cost: _____

Date installed: _____

STYLISH SHELVES

Bookshelves are meant to hold books, but that doesn't mean they can't be stylish as well. Try these six simple steps to add flair to your shelves:

➤ Use boxes, baskets, and other containers to hold loose items and small books. They add texture and color, and keep your shelves in order.

➤ Try restricting your range of colors. Choose a few hues and stick to them. You may need to remove book jackets to make the books fit into your color scheme.

➤ Balance shapes as well as colors. Stack large books horizontally and place them next to vertically stacked books. Offset the hard lines of the books with round shapes, like bowls and plates.

➤ Display your collections. Add shells, figurines, and photographs to break up the monotony of the books.

➤ Make space to breathe. Fill each shelf as needed, but allow space between books and objects so the look isn't overwhelming.

➤ Add life. Whether you prefer live plants, dried flowers, or family photos, include reminders of the living world.

WINDOW TREATMENTS

Window location: _____

    Measurements

        Height: _____ Width: _____

        Top of window to floor: _____

    Type of treatment: _____

        Height: _____ Width: _____

        Purchased from: _____ Date: _____ Cost:_____

        Date installed: _____

WALL COVERING

Wall measurements

    North: _____ South: _____

    East: _____ West: _____

Brand: _____

Pattern: _____

Color and number: _____

Purchased from: _____ Date: _____ Cost: _____

Date installed: _____

OFFICE FURNITURE AND FIXTURES				
ITEM	PURCHASED FROM	DATE	COST	COMMENTS

FAMILY ROOM

FLOOR COVERING

Floor measurements: _____

Type of floor: _____

    Brand: _____

    Color: _____ Pattern: _____

Type of backing: _____

Purchased from: _____ Date: _____ Cost:_____

Date installed: _____

WINDOW TREATMENTS

Window location: _____

    Measurements

        Height: _____ Width: _____

        Top of window to floor: _____

    Type of treatment: _____

        Height: _____ Width: _____

        Purchased from: _____ Date: _____ Cost:_____

        Date installed: _____

Window location: _____

    Measurements

        Height: _____ Width: _____

        Top of window to floor: _____

    Type of treatment: _____

        Height: _____ Width: _____

        Purchased from: _____ Date: _____ Cost:_____

        Date installed: _____

WALL COVERING

Wall measurements

    North: _____ South: _____

    East: _____ West: _____

Brand: _____

Pattern: _____

Color and number: _____

Purchased from: _____ Date: _____ Cost:_____

Date installed: _____

FAMILY ROOM FURNITURE AND FIXTURES				
ITEM	PURCHASED FROM	DATE	COST	COMMENTS

CUSTOM CARPETING

Design your own carpet by using modular pieces—big squares with adhesive backs. Use two complementary colors to create an attractive border or a lively checkerboard pattern.

HALLWAY/STAIRWAY #1

FLOOR COVERING

Floor measurements: _____

Type of floor: _____

    Brand: _____

    Color: _____ Pattern: _____

Type of backing: _____

Purchased from: _____ Date: _____ Cost: _____

Date installed: _____

WINDOW TREATMENTS

Window location: _____

    Measurements

        Height: _____ Width: _____

        Top of window to floor: _____

    Type of treatment: _____

        Height: _____ Width: _____

        Purchased from: _____ Date: _____ Cost:_____

        Date installed: _____

WALL COVERING

Wall measurements

    North: _____ South: _____

    East: _____ West: _____

Brand: _____

Pattern: _____

Color and number: _____

Purchased from: _____ Date: _____ Cost: _____

Date installed: _____

HALLWAY/STAIRWAY #1 FURNITURE AND FIXTURES				
ITEM	PURCHASED FROM	DATE	COST	COMMENTS

HALLWAY/STAIRWAY #2

FLOOR COVERING

Floor measurements: _____

Type of floor: _____

    Brand: _____

    Color: _____ Pattern: _____

Type of backing: _____

Purchased from: _____ Date: _____ Cost: _____

Date installed: _____

WINDOW TREATMENTS

Window location: _____

    Measurements

        Height: _____ Width: _____

        Top of window to floor: _____

    Type of treatment: _____

        Height: _____ Width: _____

        Purchased from: _____ Date: _____ Cost: _____

        Date installed: _____

WALL COVERING

Wall measurements

    North: _____ South: _____

    East: _____ West: _____

Brand: _____

Pattern: _____

Color and number: _____

Purchased from: _____ Date: _____ Cost: _____

Date installed: _____

COLOR CONTRASTS

Create a strong visual impact in an overlooked space by setting simple white furniture, such as a chair or a table, against a brightly colored wall.

HALLWAY/STAIRWAY #2 FURNITURE AND FIXTURES				
ITEM	PURCHASED FROM	DATE	COST	COMMENTS

Notes

Vacations, Celebrations, and Entertaining

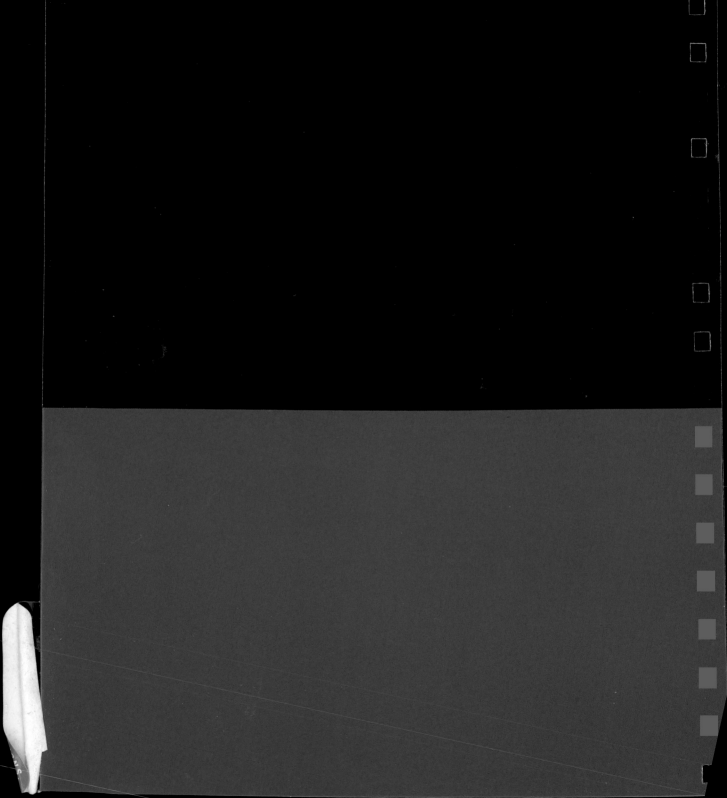

Vacations, Celebrations, and Entertaining

This section provides space to record important information you need to remember about vacations and holidays. It's also the place to bring back warm memories of vacations and holidays past and to help you plan exciting days to come. This is where you'll write down vital information about your passport, keep track of the hotels and restaurants you want to visit again, and record frequent flyer membership numbers. You'll prepare for upcoming birthdays and holidays with ease after filling out the table noting birthdates, gift ideas and preferences, the list of holiday cards sent and received, and notes on entertaining ideas that have worked well in the past. Keep in the pocket a copy of your passport ID page (give one to family members or friends when you travel, in case your passport is lost or stolen) along with frequent flyer cards and the phone number of your favorite florist. Then you'll have smooth sailing ahead.

Vacations

CONTACT INFORMATION

FREQUENT FLYER MEMBERSHIPS

Airline: _____

    Phone number: _____ E-mail address: _____

    Membership number: _____

Airline: _____

    Phone number: _____ E-mail address: _____

    Membership number: _____

Airline: _____

    Phone number: _____ E-mail address: _____

    Membership number: _____

TRAVEL AGENCY: _____

Agent: _____

    Phone number: _____ Cell phone number: _____

    Fax number: _____ E-mail address: _____

    Address: _____

TRAVEL CLUBS: _____

Automobile club: _____

    Roadside assistance phone number: _____

    Other services phone number: _____

    Membership number: _____ Expiration date: _____

Other: _____

    Phone number: _____

    Membership number: _____ Expiration date: _____

Other: _____

    Phone number: _____

    Membership number: _____ Expiration date: _____

OTHER: _____

    Phone number: _____ Cell phone number: _____

    Fax number: _____ E-mail address: _____

    Address: _____

OTHER: _____

    Phone number: _____ Cell phone number: _____

    Fax number: _____ E-mail address: _____

    Address: _____

PASSPORT INFORMATION

NATIONAL PASSPORT INFORMATION CENTER: 1-877-487-2778

PASSPORT HOLDER: _____

    Passport number: _____ Expiration date: _____

PASSPORT HOLDER: _____

    Passport number: _____ Expiration date: _____

PASSPORT HOLDER: _____

    Passport number: _____ Expiration date: _____

PASSPORT HOLDER: _____

    Passport number: _____ Expiration date: _____

PASSPORT HOLDER: _____

    Passport number: _____ Expiration date: _____

FAVORITE HOTELS AND RESTAURANTS

DESTINATION: _____

    Hotel: _____

        Phone number: _____ Fax number: _____

        Address: _____

        E-mail address: _____

    Restaurant: _____

        Phone number: _____ E-mail address: _____

        Address: _____

Restaurant: _____

    Phone number: _____ E-mail address: _____

    Address: _____

Other (museums, parks, and so on): _____

    Phone number: _____ E-mail address: _____

    Address: _____

Other (museums, parks, and so on): _____

    Phone number: _____ E-mail address: _____

    Address: _____

DESTINATION: _____

Hotel: _____

    Phone number: _____ Fax number: _____

    Address: _____

    E-mail address: _____

Restaurant: _____

    Phone number: _____ E-mail address: _____

    Address: _____

Restaurant: _____

    Phone number: _____ E-mail address: _____

    Address: _____

Other (museums, parks, and so on): _____

    Phone number: _____ E-mail address: _____

    Address: _____

Other (museums, parks, and so on): _____

    Phone number: _____ E-mail address: _____

    Address: _____

DESTINATION: _____

Hotel: _____

    Phone number: _____ Fax number: _____

    Address: _____

    E-mail address: _____

Restaurant: _____

    Phone number: _____ E-mail address: _____

    Address: _____

Restaurant: _____

    Phone number: _____ E-mail address: _____

    Address: _____

Other (museums, parks, and so on): _____

    Phone number: _____ E-mail address: _____

    Address: _____

Other (museums, parks, and so on): _____

    Phone number: _____ E-mail address: _____

    Address: _____

VACATION CARE

Going on vacation is wonderful, but getting sick on vacation isn't. And trying to find a local doctor can make you feel even worse. Use the following advice to make sure you're in good hands, no matter where you are:

➤ For true emergencies, such as non-stop bleeding, go immediately to the nearest emergency room. In the United States, call 911 for chest pain.

➤ For lesser health concerns, call your family physician and ask if he or she can recommend a colleague where you're traveling. Better yet, ask your doctor this question before you leave for your trip.

➤ Call the referral service of the nearest university hospital; doctors affiliated with medical schools may be more highly qualified than someone chosen at random.

➤ For treatment after hours, try a university hospital's urgent-care center.

FAVORITE DAY TRIPS:

_____

_____

_____

_____

_____

_____

_____

_____

Celebrations 🎁

BIRTHDAYS AND ANNIVERSARIES

Use the table below to remember whose birthday and/or anniversary falls on which day.

MONTH	DAY	NAME	BIRTHDAY OR ANNIVERSARY
JANUARY			
FEBRUARY			
MARCH			
APRIL			

MONTH	DAY	NAME	BIRTHDAY OR ANNIVERSARY
MAY			
JUNE			
JULY			
AUGUST			
SEPTEMBER			

MONTH	DAY	NAME	BIRTHDAY OR ANNIVERSARY
OCTOBER			
NOVEMBER			
DECEMBER			

CANDLEHOLDERS GOOD ENOUGH TO EAT

Make a birthday cupcake extra-special by placing the birthday candle through the hole of a Life Savers candy. Or drop a dollop of colorful icing on the cupcake, stick a candle in the middle of it, and enjoy both the candle and the candleholder.

PUMPKIN MAKEOVER

Tired of carving the same face on your Halloween pumpkin year after year? Try adding some style to your creation with materials from your yard. Make cat-eye glasses with spiky leaves, lovely long eyelashes with thin twigs, and a fabulous hairdo with moss. Your pumpkin will be the envy of the neighborhood.

GIFT LIST

Jot down ideas for gifts for friends and family as you think of them throughout the year.

NAME	GIFT IDEAS/PREFERENCES	SIZES

HOLIDAY CARDS

There's no need to rack your brains to remember if you received a holiday card from a particular friend last year—or if you sent her one yourself—if you record that information in this handy table as you send and receive cards. You may want to photocopy these pages so you can use them in years to come.

YEAR _____

NAME	SENT	REC'D

NAME	SENT	REC'D

Entertaining

CONTACT INFORMATION

FLORIST: _____

    Phone number: _____ Cell phone number: _____

    Fax number: _____ E-mail address: _____

    Address: _____

CATERER: _____

    Phone number: _____ Cell phone number: _____

    Fax number: _____ E-mail address: _____

    Address: _____

PARTY HELPERS (BARTENDERS, WAITERS, CLEAN UP STAFF, AND SO ON):

Type of helper: _____

    Phone number: _____ Cell phone number: _____

    Fax number: _____ E-mail address: _____

    Address: _____

Type of helper: _____

    Phone number: _____ Cell phone number: _____

    Fax number: _____ E-mail address: _____

    Address: _____

Type of helper: _____

    Phone number: _____ Cell phone number: _____

    Fax number: _____ E-mail address: _____

    Address: _____

TABLE TREATS

No matter what the occasion—a birthday celebration, a baby shower, or a Mother's Day tea—plants make any event even more memorable. Write each guest's name on a wooden craft stick, and place the stick in a small flowering plant. Use these potted plants as unusual place cards, and suggest guests take them home as reminders of their special day.

PARTY RENTALS (TABLES, CHAIRS, COAT RACKS, AND SO ON):

_____

Phone number: _____ Cell phone number: _____

Fax number: _____ E-mail address: _____

Address: _____

OTHER: _____

Phone number: _____ Cell phone number: _____

Fax number: _____ E-mail address: _____

Address: _____

OTHER: _____

Phone number: _____ Cell phone number: _____

Fax number: _____ E-mail address: _____

Address: _____

OTHER: _____

Phone number: _____ Cell phone number: _____

Fax number: _____ E-mail address: _____

Address: _____

EASY ENTERTAINING

Stick fake, colorful jewels (found at craft stores) onto inexpensive plastic glasses; they'll immediately add pizzazz to your drinks. Once the party's over, simply toss or recycle the plastic cups.

ENTERTAINING FAVORITES

DRINKS

Beer: _____

Champagne: _____

Red wine: _____

White wine: _____

Other: _____

FOOD

Appetizers: _____

_____

_____

_____

Main dishes: _____

_____

_____

_____

_____

Side dishes: _____

_____

_____

_____

Desserts: _____

_____

_____

_____

TABLE DECORATIONS

_____

_____

_____

PARTY TIMETABLE

Use this timetable as a checklist to plan a big party:

FOUR WEEKS AHEAD

☐ Mail, e-mail, or deliver the invitations. Do not rely on the telephone or word of mouth.

☐ Keep a written guest list.

☐ Plan the menu.

☐ Check on cooking and serving equipment. Rent or buy what may be needed.

☐ If needed, arrange for help with parking, serving, or cleanup, and rent coat racks.

THREE WEEKS AHEAD

- [ ] Buy nonperishables, disposable items, liquor, nonalcoholic beverages, and mixers.
- [ ] Plan traffic flow and table service.
- [ ] Clean and iron the linens.
- [ ] Order any grocery or butcher items.

TWO WEEKS AHEAD

- [ ] Cook and freeze foods such as desserts, breads, and casseroles.
- [ ] Check the condition of the garden if the party is to be outdoors.
- [ ] Do any major housecleaning.
- [ ] Polish silver if needed.
- [ ] Begin making ice.
- [ ] Order flowers.

TWO DAYS AHEAD

- [ ] Set the buffet table.
- [ ] Set up the bar.
- [ ] Set up the music.
- [ ] Clean the rooms where the party will be held, and rearrange furniture as necessary.
- [ ] Begin making food or portions of recipes such as pasta or potato salads, crudité dips, and some desserts.
- [ ] Post a last-minute itemized checklist.
- [ ] Label platters and set out serving utensils.

ONE DAY AHEAD

- [ ] Draw a timetable of what needs to be cooked and served when.
- [ ] Shop for perishable foods.
- [ ] Do bulk of cooking.
- [ ] Pick up and arrange flowers.
- [ ] Call all helpers and give each explicit instructions.
- [ ] Make the punch base.

DAY OF THE PARTY

- [ ] Finish cooking.
- [ ] Arrange ice and fruit for the bar.

Notes

Maintenance
and Repair

Maintenance and Repair

Keeping your home running smoothly means maintaining and repairing the physical structure—the actual house—as well as what's inside it. That also means keeping track of lots of details, from names and numbers of the roofer, the painter, and the electrician to the warranty information on your dishwasher to where to turn off the water when you go on vacation. You also need to record improvements you've made to your home—new windows or a new roof, for example—because you'll need that information when you sell your house. This section provides the space for you to keep track of it all. Keep business cards of home repair professionals and receipts and warranties for appliances in the pocket.

Your Smooth Running Home ⌐———

CONTACT INFORMATION

AIR CONDITIONING INSTALLATION AND REPAIR: _____

    Phone number: _____ Cell phone number: _____

    Fax number: _____ E-mail address: _____

    Address: _____

    Date of service: _____ Cost: _____

      Work done: _____

    (For model number, warranty information, and service details, *see page 117.*)

ALARM SYSTEM INSTALLATION AND MAINTENANCE: _____

    Phone number: _____ Cell phone number: _____

    Fax number: _____ E-mail address: _____

    Address: _____

    Date of service: _____ Cost: _____

      Work done: _____

CARPENTER: _____

    Phone number: _____ Cell phone number: _____

    Fax number: _____ E-mail address: _____

    Address: _____

    Date of service: _____ Cost: _____

      Work done: _____

CHIMNEY CLEANING AND REPAIR: _____

    Phone number: _____ Cell phone number: _____

    Fax number: _____ E-mail address: _____

HOT, COLD, HOT, COLD

Are your air conditioning bills heating you up? Try raising the thermostat on the air conditioner. You'll save up to 3 percent per month in energy costs for every degree above 72° F.

Address: _____

Date of service: _____ Cost: _____

   Work done: _____

CONTRACTOR: _____

   Phone number: _____ Cell phone number: _____

   Fax number: _____ E-mail address: _____

   Address: _____

   Date of service: _____ Cost: _____

    Work done: _____

CONTRACTOR: _____

   Phone number: _____ Cell phone number: _____

   Fax number: _____ E-mail address: _____

   Address: _____

   Date of service: _____ Cost: _____

    Work done: _____

DRIVEWAY CONTRACTOR AND REPAIR: _____

   Phone number: _____ Cell phone number: _____

   Fax number: _____ E-mail address: _____

   Address: _____

   Date of service: _____ Cost: _____

    Work done: _____

ELECTRICIAN: _____

   Phone number: _____ Cell phone number: _____

   Fax number: _____ E-mail address: _____

FIX IT UP . . . WHEN?

Do you know the best times to spruce up or remodel your home? Try painting in the fall, or whenever your area sees quiet weather and little rain. Think about remodeling your bathroom in the winter when contractors aren't overwhelmed with work. They'll get the job done faster and possibly for less than you'd pay in the summer.

Address: _____

Date of service: _____ Cost: _____

  Work done: _____

EXTERMINATOR/PEST CONTROL: _____

  Phone number: _____ Cell phone number: _____

  Fax number: _____ E-mail address: _____

  Address: _____

  Date of service: _____ Cost: _____

    Work done: _____

FURNACE MAINTENANCE AND REPAIR: _____

  Phone number: _____ Cell phone number: _____

  Fax number: _____ E-mail address: _____

  Address: _____

  Date of service: _____ Cost: _____

    Work done: _____

  (For model number, warranty information, and service details, *see page 122.*)

GARAGE DOOR SERVICE AND REPAIR: _____

  Phone number: _____ Cell phone number: _____

  Fax number: _____ E-mail address: _____

  Address: _____

  Date of service: _____ Cost: _____

    Work done: _____

GUTTER CLEANING SERVICE: _____

  Phone number: _____ Cell phone number: _____

  Fax number: _____ E-mail address: _____

  Address: _____

  Date of service: _____ Cost: _____

    Work done: _____

HANDYMAN: _____

    Phone number: _____ Cell phone number: _____

    Fax number: _____ E-mail address: _____

    Address: _____

    Date of service: _____ Cost: _____

      Work done: _____

LOCKSMITH: _____

    Phone number: _____ Cell phone number: _____

    Fax number: _____ E-mail address: _____

    Address: _____

    Date of service: _____ Cost: _____

      Work done: _____

MASON: _____

    Phone number: _____ Cell phone number: _____

    Fax number: _____ E-mail address: _____

    Address: _____

    Date of service: _____ Cost: _____

      Work done: _____

MOLD TREATMENT: _____

    Phone number: _____ Cell phone number: _____

    Fax number: _____ E-mail address: _____

    Address: _____

    Date of service: _____ Cost: _____

      Work done: _____

PAINTER (EXTERIOR): _____

    Phone number: _____ Cell phone number: _____

    Fax number: _____ E-mail address: _____

    Address: _____

Date of service: _____ Cost: _____

   Work done: _____

PAINTER (INTERIOR): _____

Phone number: _____ Cell phone number: _____

Fax number: _____ E-mail address: _____

Address: _____

Date of service: _____ Cost: _____

   Work done: _____

PIANO TUNER: _____

Phone number: _____ Cell phone number: _____

Fax number: _____ E-mail address: _____

Address: _____

Date of service: _____ Cost: _____

   Work done: _____

PLUMBER: _____

Phone number: _____ Cell phone number: _____

Fax number: _____ E-mail address: _____

Address: _____

Date of service: _____ Cost: _____

   Work done: _____

POWER WASHER: _____

Phone number: _____ Cell phone number: _____

Fax number: _____ E-mail address: _____

Address: _____

Date of service: _____ Cost: _____

   Work done: _____

RADON TREATMENT: _____

    Phone number: _____ Cell phone number: _____

    Fax number: _____ E-mail address: _____

    Address: _____

    Date of service: _____ Cost: _____

      Work done: _____

ROOFER: _____

    Phone number: _____ Cell phone number: _____

    Fax number: _____ E-mail address: _____

    Address: _____

    Date of service: _____ Cost: _____

      Work done: _____

SEWER/CESSPOOL/SEPTIC SYSTEM MAINTENANCE: _____

    Phone number: _____ Cell phone number: _____

    Fax number: _____ E-mail address: _____

    Address: _____

    Date of service: _____ Cost: _____

      Work done: _____

SNOW REMOVAL SERVICE: _____

    Phone number: _____ Cell phone number: _____

    Fax number: _____ E-mail address: _____

    Address: _____

    Date of service contract: _____ Cost: _____

      Work to be done: _____

SPRINKLER MAINTENANCE AND REPAIR: _See Garden and Yard, page 140._

OTHER: _____

    Phone number: _____ Cell phone number: _____

Fax number: _____ E-mail address: _____

Address: _____

Date of service: _____ Cost: _____

   Work done: _____

OTHER: _____

   Phone number: _____ Cell phone number: _____

   Fax number: _____ E-mail address: _____

   Address: _____

   Date of service: _____ Cost: _____

      Work done: _____

OTHER: _____

   Phone number: _____ Cell phone number: _____

   Fax number: _____ E-mail address: _____

   Address: _____

   Date of service: _____ Cost: _____

      Work done: _____

UTILITIES

Use the following space to record phone numbers, account numbers, and more so you'll
have all the information you need next time you have a question or need a repair.

CABLE COMPANY/SATELLITE COMPANY: _____

   Customer service phone number: _____

   Billing phone number: _____

   Repair phone number: _____

   Address: _____

   Account number: _____

CELLULAR PHONE SERVICE: _____

   Customer service phone number: _____

   Billing phone number: _____

Repair phone number: _____

Address: _____

Account number: _____

Date of service contract: _____

Contract expiration date: _____

ELECTRIC COMPANY: _____

Customer service phone number: _____

Billing phone number: _____

Repair phone number: _____

Address: _____

Account number: _____

GAS COMPANY: _____

Customer service phone number: _____

Billing phone number: _____

Repair phone number: _____

Address: _____

Account number: _____

OIL COMPANY: _____

Customer service phone number: _____

Billing phone number: _____

Repair phone number: _____

Address: _____

Account number: _____

TELEPHONE COMPANY (LOCAL): _____

Customer service phone number: _____

Billing phone number: _____

Repair phone number: _____

Address: _____

Account number: _____

TELEPHONE COMPANY (LONG DISTANCE): _____

    Customer service phone number: _____

    Billing phone number: _____

    Repair phone number: _____

    Address: _____

    Account number: _____

WATER COMPANY:

    Customer service phone number: _____

    Billing phone number: _____

    Repair phone number: _____

    Address: _____

    Account number: _____

OTHER: _____

    Customer service phone number: _____

    Billing phone number: _____

    Repair phone number: _____

    Address: _____

    Account number: _____

OTHER: _____

    Customer service phone number: _____

    Billing phone number: _____

    Repair phone number: _____

    Address: _____

    Account number: _____

OTHER: _____

    Customer service phone number: _____

    Billing phone number: _____

    Repair phone number: _____

Address: _____

Account number: _____

UTILITIES ACCESS INFORMATION

You should always know where you can turn on and off your utilities and more in case of an emergency. Record that information below.

ELECTRICITY: _____

FURNACE/BOILER: _____

GAS: _____

HOT WATER HEATER: _____

WATER: _____

APPLIANCES AND MORE

Use the following space to record important information about the equipment you use on a regular basis.

AIR CONDITIONING (CENTRAL AIR)

Manufacturer: _____

Customer service phone number: _____

Model number: _____ Serial number: _____

Purchased from: _____

Date of purchase: _____

Warranty (yes/no)? _____ Date of expiration: _____

Service and repair: _____

Phone number: _____

Address: _____

Date of service: _____ Cost: _____

Repairs made: _____

Air conditioning (unit)

Manufacturer: _____

Customer service phone number: _____

Model number: _____ Serial number: _____

Purchased from: _____

Date of purchase: _____

Warranty (yes/no)? _____ Date of expiration: _____

Service and repair: _____

    Phone number: _____

    Address: _____

    Date of service: _____ Cost: _____

    Repairs made: _____

Air conditioning (unit)

Manufacturer: _____

Customer service phone number: _____

Model number: _____ Serial number: _____

Purchased from: _____

Date of purchase: _____

Warranty (yes/no)? _____ Date of expiration: _____

Service and repair: _____

    Phone number: _____

    Address: _____

    Date of service: _____ Cost: _____

    Repairs made: _____

Attic fan

Manufacturer: _____

Customer service phone number: _____

Model number: _____ Serial number: _____

Purchased from: _____

Date of purchase: _____

Warranty (yes/no)? _____ Date of expiration: _____

Service and repair: _____

  Phone number: _____

  Address: _____

  Date of service: _____ Cost: _____

  Repairs made: _____

CEILING FAN

  Manufacturer: _____

  Customer service phone number: _____

  Model number: _____ Serial number: _____

  Purchased from: _____

  Date of purchase: _____

  Warranty (yes/no)? _____ Date of expiration: _____

  Service and repair: _____

    Phone number: _____

    Address: _____

    Date of service: _____ Cost: _____

    Repairs made: _____

COOKTOP

  Manufacturer: _____

  Customer service phone number: _____

  Model number: _____ Serial number: _____

  Purchased from: _____

  Date of purchase: _____

  Warranty (yes/no)? _____ Date of expiration: _____

  Service and repair: _____

    Phone number: _____

    Address: _____

    Date of service: _____ Cost: _____

    Repairs made: _____

DEHUMIDIFIER

Manufacturer: _____

Customer service phone number: _____

Model number: _____ Serial number: _____

Purchased from: _____

Date of purchase: _____

Warranty (yes/no)? _____ Date of expiration: _____

Service and repair: _____

   Phone number: _____

   Address: _____

   Date of service: _____ Cost: _____

   Repairs made: _____

DISHWASHER

Manufacturer: _____

Customer service phone number: _____

Model number: _____ Serial number: _____

Purchased from: _____

Date of purchase: _____

Warranty (yes/no)? _____ Date of expiration: _____

Service and repair: _____

   Phone number: _____

   Address: _____

   Date of service: _____ Cost: _____

   Repairs made: _____

DISPOSAL

Manufacturer: _____

Customer service phone number: _____

Model number: _____ Serial number: _____

Purchased from: _____

Date of purchase: _____

Warranty (yes/no)? _____ Date of expiration: _____

Service and repair: _____

  Phone number: _____

  Address: _____

  Date of service: _____ Cost: _____

  Repairs made: _____

Dryer

  Manufacturer: _____

  Customer service phone number: _____

  Model number: _____ Serial number: _____

  Purchased from: _____

  Date of purchase: _____

  Warranty (yes/no)? _____ Date of expiration: _____

  Service and repair: _____

    Phone number: _____

    Address: _____

    Date of service: _____ Cost: _____

    Repairs made: _____

Freezer

  Manufacturer: _____

  Customer service phone number: _____

  Model number: _____ Serial number: _____

  Purchased from: _____

  Date of purchase: _____

  Warranty (yes/no)? _____ Date of expiration: _____

  Service and repair: _____

    Phone number: _____

    Address: _____

    Date of service: _____ Cost: _____

    Repairs made: _____

LET IT SNOW!

Winterize your house with these three easy tips to save yourself from costly repairs and a miserably cold house:

➤ Have your heating system checked once a year by a professional—ideally, before the cold weather hits. This can help slash your monthly heating bill.

➤ Check for holes or gaps in your walls, windows, doors, and even your foundation. Seal every crack and crevice, and you could save up to 35 percent on your heating bill.

➤ Make sure you don't have any exposed pipes in unheated areas of your house. If you do, get them insulated immediately so they won't freeze and burst.

FURNACE

Manufacturer: _____

Customer service phone number: _____

Model number: _____ Serial number: _____

Purchased from: _____

Date of purchase: _____

Warranty (yes/no)? _____ Date of expiration: _____

Service and repair: _____

   Phone number: _____

   Address: _____

   Date of service: _____ Cost: _____

   Repairs made: _____

GENERATOR

Manufacturer: _____

Customer service phone number: _____

Model number: _____ Serial number: _____

Purchased from: _____

Date of purchase: _____

Warranty (yes/no)? _____ Date of expiration: _____

Service and repair: _____

   Phone number: _____

   Address: _____

   Date of service: _____ Cost: _____

   Repairs made: _____

HUMIDIFIER

Manufacturer: _____

Customer service phone number: _____

Model number: _____ Serial number: _____

Purchased from: _____

Date of purchase: _____

Warranty (yes/no)? _____ Date of expiration: _____

Service and repair: _____

Phone number: _____

Address: _____

Date of service: _____ Cost: _____

Repairs made: _____

MICROWAVE OVEN

Manufacturer: _____

Customer service phone number: _____

Model number: _____ Serial number: _____

Purchased from: _____

Date of purchase: _____

Warranty (yes/no)? _____ Date of expiration: _____

Service and repair: _____

Phone number: _____

Address: _____

Date of service: _____ Cost: _____

Repairs made: _____

OVEN/STOVE

Manufacturer: _____

Customer service phone number: _____

Model number: _____ Serial number: _____

Purchased from: _____

Date of purchase: _____

Warranty (yes/no)? _____ Date of expiration: _____

Service and repair: _____

    Phone number: _____

    Address: _____

    Date of service: _____ Cost: _____

    Repairs made: _____

REFRIGERATOR TIPS

These three simple tips will help keep the refrigerator repairman away:

➤ Every six months, vacuum the condenser coils under the refrigerator. Unplug the refrigerator first, then snap off the grate covering the coils. If you have pets, be sure to clean the condenser coils more often.

➤ Maintain the rubbery gasket around the refrigerator door by wiping it down every month. For extra protection against costly repairs, rub the hinge side with petroleum jelly.

➤ Keep your freezer from working overtime by keeping it full. Put plastic containers of water in the freezer if it's empty.

REFRIGERATOR

    Manufacturer: _____

    Customer service phone number: _____

    Model number: _____ Serial number: _____

    Purchased from: _____

    Date of purchase: _____

    Warranty (yes/no)? _____ Date of expiration: _____

    Service and repair: _____

      Phone number: _____

      Address: _____

      Date of service: _____ Cost: _____

      Repairs made: _____

SUMP PUMP

    Manufacturer: _____

    Customer service phone number: _____

    Model number: _____ Serial number: _____

Purchased from: _____

Date of purchase: _____

Warranty (yes/no)? _____ Date of expiration: _____

Service and repair: _____

   Phone number: _____

   Address: _____

   Date of service: _____ Cost: _____

   Repairs made: _____

VACUUM CLEANER:

   Manufacturer: _____

   Customer service phone number: _____

   Model number: _____ Serial number: _____

   Purchased from: _____

   Date of purchase: _____

   Warranty (yes/no)? _____ Date of expiration: _____

   Service and repair: _____

      Phone number: _____

      Address: _____

      Date of service: _____ Cost: _____

      Repairs made: _____

WASHING MACHINE

   Manufacturer: _____

   Customer service phone number: _____

   Model number: _____ Serial number: _____

   Purchased from: _____

   Date of purchase: _____

   Warranty (yes/no)? _____ Date of expiration: _____

   Service and repair: _____

   Phone number: _____

   Address: _____

Date of service: _____ Cost: _____

Repairs made: _____

WATER HEATER

Manufacturer: _____

Customer service phone number: _____ _____

Model number: _____ Serial number: _____

Purchased from: _____

Date of purchase: _____

Warranty (yes/no)? _____ Date of expiration: _____

Service and repair: _____

  Phone number: _____

  Address: _____

  Date of service: _____ Cost: _____

  Repairs made: _____

CODDLE YOUR WATER HEATER

Wrap your water heater in an insulation blanket; you'll lower the cost of running it by up to 9 percent.

OTHER: _____

Manufacturer: _____

Customer service phone number: _____

Model number: _____ Serial number: _____

Purchased from: _____

Date of purchase: _____

Warranty (yes/no)? _____ Date of expiration: _____

Service and repair: _____

  Phone number: _____

  Address: _____

  Date of service: _____ Cost: _____

  Repairs made: _____

Home Office, Communication, and Entertainment 📺

HOME OFFICE

COMPUTER

ANTIVIRUS INFORMATION

Antivirus software: _____

Product key: _____

Date installed: _____ Renewal date: _____

Online customer service: _____

Online technical support: _____

Customer service phone number: _____

Technical support phone number: _____

HARDWARE

Manufacturer: _____ Model number: _____

Service tag number: _____ Service code number: _____

Purchased from: _____ Date: _____

Warranty (yes/no)? _____ Date of expiration: _____

Online customer service: _____

Online technical support: _____

Customer service phone number: _____

Technical support phone number: _____

HARDWARE ADD-ONS

_____

_____

_____

_____

_____

INTERNET SERVICE PROVIDER: _____

Screen names: _____

_____

_____

Online customer service: _____

Online technical support: _____

Customer service phone number: _____

Technical support phone number: _____

PRINTER

Manufacturer: _____ Model number: _____

Purchased from: _____ Date: _____

Warranty (yes/no)? _____ Date of expiration: _____

Online customer service: _____

Online technical support: _____

Customer service phone number: _____

Technical support phone number: _____

SERVICE AND REPAIR COMPANY: _____

Phone number: _____ Cell phone number: _____

Fax number: _____ E-mail address: _____

Address: _____

Date of service: _____ Cost: _____

Work done: _____

_____

_____

SPYWARE INFORMATION

Spyware software: _____

Product key: _____

Date installed: _____ Renewal date: _____

Online customer service: _____

Online technical support: _____

Customer service phone number: _____

Technical support phone number: _____

OTHER: _____

_____

_____

_____

_____

_____

_____

OTHER OFFICE EQUIPMENT

FAX MACHINE

Manufacturer: _____

Model number: _____ Serial number: _____

Customer service phone number: _____

Purchased from: _____ Date: _____

Warranty (yes/no)? _____ Date of expiration: _____

TELEPHONE

Manufacturer: _____

Model number: _____ Serial number: _____

Customer service phone number: _____

Purchased from: _____ Date: _____

Warranty (yes/no)? _____ Date of expiration: _____

TELEPHONE ANSWERING MACHINE

Manufacturer: _____

Model number: _____ Serial number: _____

Customer service phone number: _____

Purchased from: _____ Date: _____

Warranty (yes/no)? _____Date of expiration: _____

OTHER: _____

Manufacturer: _____

Model number: _____ Serial number: _____

Customer service phone number: _____

Purchased from: _____ Date: _____

Warranty (yes/no)? _____Date of expiration: _____

OTHER: _____

Manufacturer: _____

Model number: _____ Serial number: _____

Customer service phone number: _____

Purchased from: _____ Date: _____

Warranty (yes/no)? _____Date of expiration: _____

COMMUNICATION
(FAMILY PHONES AND COMPUTERS)

CELL PHONE

Manufacturer: _____

Model number: _____ Serial number: _____

Customer service phone number: _____

Purchased from: _____ Date: _____

Warranty (yes/no)? _____Date of expiration: _____

CELL PHONE

Manufacturer: _____

Model number: _____ Serial number: _____

Customer service phone number: _____

Purchased from: _____ Date: _____

Warranty (yes/no)? _____ Date of expiration: _____

COMPUTER (FAMILY COMPUTER)

Manufacturer: _____

Customer service phone number: _____

Model number: _____ Serial number: _____

Service tag number: _____ Service code number: _____

Purchased from: _____ Date: _____

Warranty (yes/no)? _____ Date of expiration: _____

TELEPHONE

Manufacturer: _____

Model number: _____ Serial number: _____

Customer service phone number: _____

Purchased from: _____ Date: _____

Warranty (yes/no)? _____ Date of expiration: _____

TELEPHONE

Manufacturer: _____

Model number: _____ Serial number: _____

Customer service phone number: _____

Purchased from: _____ Date: _____

Warranty (yes/no)? _____ Date of expiration: _____

TELEPHONE ANSWERING MACHINE

Manufacturer: _____

Model number: _____ Serial number: _____

Customer service phone number: _____

Purchased from: _____ Date: _____

Warranty (yes/no)? _____ Date of expiration: _____

OTHER: _____

    Manufacturer: _____

    Model number: _____ Serial number: _____

    Customer service phone number: _____

    Purchased from: _____ Date: _____

    Warranty (yes/no)? _____Date of expiration: _____

OTHER: _____

    Manufacturer: _____

    Model number: _____ Serial number: _____

    Customer service phone number: _____

    Purchased from: _____ Date: _____

    Warranty (yes/no)? _____Date of expiration: _____

ENTERTAINMENT

CD PLAYER/RECORDER

    Manufacturer: _____

    Customer service phone number: _____

    Model number: _____ Serial number: _____

    Purchased from: _____ Date: _____

    Warranty (yes/no)? _____Date of expiration: _____

DVD PLAYER/RECORDER

    Manufacturer: _____

    Customer service phone number: _____

    Model number: _____ Serial number: _____

    Purchased from: _____ Date: _____

    Warranty (yes/no)? _____Date of expiration: _____

DVD PLAYER/RECORDER

    Manufacturer: _____

    Customer service phone number: _____

Model number: _____ Serial number: _____

Purchased from: _____ Date: _____

Warranty (yes/no)? _____ Date of expiration: _____

STEREO EQUIPMENT (COMPONENT #1)

Manufacturer: _____

Customer service phone number: _____

Model number: _____ Serial number: _____

Purchased from: _____ Date: _____

Warranty (yes/no)? _____ Date of expiration: _____

STEREO EQUIPMENT (COMPONENT #2)

Manufacturer: _____

Customer service phone number: _____

Model number: _____ Serial number: _____

Purchased from: _____ Date: _____

Warranty (yes/no)? _____ Date of expiration: _____

STEREO EQUIPMENT (COMPONENT #3)

Manufacturer: _____

Customer service phone number: _____

Model number: _____ Serial number: _____

Purchased from: _____ Date: _____

Warranty (yes/no)? _____ Date of expiration: _____

TELEVISION

Manufacturer: _____

Customer service phone number: _____

Model number: _____ Serial number: _____

Purchased from: _____ Date: _____

Warranty (yes/no)? _____ Date of expiration: _____

TELEVISION

Manufacturer: _____

Customer service phone number: _____

Model number: _____ Serial number: _____

Purchased from: _____ Date: _____

Warranty (yes/no)? _____Date of expiration: _____

VCR

Manufacturer: _____

Customer service phone number: _____

Model number: _____ Serial number: _____

Purchased from: _____ Date: _____

Warranty (yes/no)? _____Date of expiration: _____

VCR

Manufacturer: _____

Customer service phone number: _____

Model number: _____ Serial number: _____

Purchased from: _____ Date: _____

Warranty (yes/no)? _____Date of expiration: _____

OTHER: _____

Manufacturer: _____

Customer service phone number: _____

Model number: _____ Serial number: _____

Purchased from: _____ Date: _____

Warranty (yes/no)? _____Date of expiration: _____

HOME IMPROVEMENTS

Be sure to record any major improvements you make to your home—new windows or a renovated bathroom, for example—because you'll need this information for tax purposes when you sell your home. It's much easier to record it all here, rather than hunt it down later. Be sure to keep the receipts for all your home improvements in a safe place.

IMPROVEMENT	DATE.	CONTRACTOR	COST	COMMENTS

CONTRACTOR CHECKLIST

Follow these four rules to protect yourself when you hire a contractor:
➤ Contact your state attorney general's office or consumer protection department—before hiring the contractor—to confirm that no complaints have been filed against the contractor.
➤ Make sure the contractor's licenses and insurance policies are current; ask to see them both.
➤ Never pay for the complete job before it starts. Put down only about 20 percent of the total bill for big renovations and only about 40 percent on small jobs.
➤ Retain a significant amount (approximately 10%) of the total bill for final payment upon your satisfaction.

Notes

_____
_____
_____
_____
_____
_____
_____
_____
_____
_____
_____
_____
_____
_____
_____
_____
_____
_____
_____
_____
_____
_____
_____
_____
_____
_____

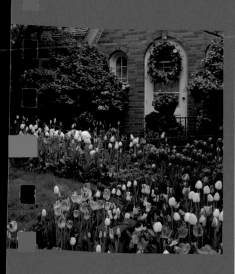

Garden and Yard

Garden and Yard

Gardening is a relaxing, enjoyable endeavor for many people, while for others it is simply a chore. The same is true of yard work. But no matter how you feel about working the soil, the fact remains that the work must get done. So whether you do the jobs yourself or hire others to do them, you need to keep track of your garden and yard equipment and services. Fill in the following information to keep your garden and yard looking their best. Keep business cards, receipts for services, and warranty information in the pocket.

Your Outdoor Living Space 🌲

CONTACT INFORMATION

LANDSCAPING COMPANY: _____

    Phone number: _____ Fax number: _____

    Address: _____

    E-mail address: _____

    Date of service: _____ Cost: _____

      Work done: _____

LAWN SERVICE (MOWING AND LEAF REMOVAL): _____

    Phone number: _____ Fax number: _____

    Address: _____

    E-mail address: _____

    Date of service: _____ Cost: _____

      Work done: _____

LAWN SERVICE (FERTILIZER/WEED AND PEST CONTROL): _____

    Phone number: _____ Fax number: _____

    Address: _____

    E-mail address: _____

    Date of service: _____ Cost: _____

      Work done: _____

NURSERY: _____

    Phone number: _____ Fax number: _____

    Address: _____

    E-mail address: _____

SPRINKLER MAINTENANCE AND REPAIR: *See Tools and Equipment, page 140.*

A LANDSCAPING LIFT

We all know new kitchens and baths help sell a house, but did you know that landscaping can help sell a house, too? Contact local real estate agents and appraisers who know your area to find out which kind of landscaping adds the most value in your neighborhood.

TREE SERVICE: _____

    Phone number: _____ Fax number: _____

    Address: _____

    E-mail address: _____

    Date of service: _____ Cost: _____

      Work done: _____

OTHER: _____

    Phone number: _____ Cell phone number: _____

    Fax number: _____ E-mail address: _____

    Address: _____

    Date of service: _____ Cost: _____

    Work done: _____

OTHER: _____

    Phone number: _____ Cell phone number: _____

    Fax number: _____ E-mail address: _____

    Address: _____

    Date of service: _____ Cost: _____

    Work done: _____

TOOLS AND EQUIPMENT

LAWN MOWER

    Manufacturer: _____

      Phone number: _____ Fax number: _____

    Model number: _____ Serial number: _____

    Purchased from: _____ Date: _____

Warranty (yes/no)? _____ Date of expiration: _____

Service and repair shop: _____

    Phone number: _____ Fax number: _____

    Address: _____

    E-mail address: _____

Date of annual maintenance check: _____

Date of other service: _____ Cost: _____

    Work done: _____

Leaf blower

Manufacturer: _____

    Phone number: _____ Fax number: _____

Model number: _____ Serial number: _____

Purchased from: _____ Date: _____

Warranty (yes/no)? _____ Date of expiration: _____

Snow blower

Manufacturer: _____

    Phone number: _____ Fax number: _____

Model number: _____ Serial number: _____

Purchased from: _____ Date: _____

Warranty (yes/no)? _____ Date of expiration: _____

Service and repair shop: _____

    Phone number: _____ Fax number: _____

    Address: _____

    E-mail address: _____

Date of service: _____ Cost: _____

    Work done: _____

Sprinkler system

Manufacturer: _____

    Phone number: _____ Fax number: _____

Model number: _____ Serial number: _____

Purchased from: _____ Date: _____

Installed by: _____

   Phone number: _____ Fax number: _____

   Address: _____

   E-mail address: _____

Date of installation: _____

Warranty (yes/no)? _____ Date of expiration: _____

Service and repair: _____

   Phone number: _____ Fax number: _____

   Address: _____

   E-mail address: _____

Date sprinklers turned on: _____ Date shut off: _____

Date of service: _____ Cost: _____

   Work done: _____

Location of sprinkler heads: _____

_____

_____

_____

_____

_____

OTHER: _____

   Manufacturer: _____

   Phone number: _____ Fax number: _____

   Model number: _____ Serial number: _____

   Purchased from: _____ Date: _____

   Warranty (yes/no)? _____ Date of expiration: _____

   Service and repair shop: _____

   Phone number: _____ Fax number: _____

   Address: _____

   E-mail address: _____

Date of service: _____ Cost: _____

    Work done: _____

OTHER: _____

    Manufacturer: _____

        Phone number: _____ Fax number: _____

    Model number: _____ Serial number: _____

    Purchased from: _____ Date: _____

    Warranty (yes/no)? _____ Date of expiration: _____

    Service and repair shop: _____

        Phone number: _____ Fax number: _____

        Address: _____

        E-mail address: _____

    Date of service: _____ Cost: _____

        Work done: _____

GAS GRILL

TYPE OF GRILL: _____

    Manufacturer: _____

        Phone number: _____ Fax number: _____

    Model number: _____ Serial number: _____

    Purchased from: _____ Date: _____

    Warranty (yes/no)? _____ Date of expiration: _____

    Service and repair shop: _____

        Phone number: _____ Fax number: _____

        Address: _____

        E-mail address: _____

    Date of service: _____ Cost: _____

        Work done: _____

Propane tank

Type: _____

Manufacturer: _____

    Phone number: _____ Fax number: _____

Model number: _____ Serial number: _____

Refill station: _____

    Phone number: _____

    Address: _____

    Cost: _____

DECK

Deck

Material (wood, synthetic, and so on): _____

Treatment (stain, paint, or other): _____

Built by: _____

    Phone number: _____ Cell phone number: _____

    Fax number: _____ E-mail address: _____

    Address: _____

    Date completed: _____ Cost: _____

Deck cleaner: _____

    Phone number: _____ Cell phone number: _____

    Fax number: _____ E-mail address: _____

    Address: _____

    Date of service: _____ Cost: _____

A BRIGHT IDEA FOR YOUR DECK

L iven up your yard by trying out a new deck stain. Put the browns and dark reds behind you and go for cheerful greens or bright reds.

DECK REPAIR: _____

    Phone number: _____ Cell phone number: _____

    Fax number: _____ E-mail address: _____

    Address: _____

    Date of service: _____ Cost: _____

      Work done: _____

BITES BE GONE

Nobody likes mosquitoes, and the fact that they're carriers of the West Nile virus has only hurt their reputation more. Follow these simple steps to avoid mosquito bites:

➤ Apply insect repellent whenever you're outside, especially during dawn, dusk, and early evening—peak biting times. When you venture out, cover yourself as best you can: Wear long pants, socks, and a long-sleeved shirt.

➤ Get rid of any standing water—in birdbaths, gutters, and flowerpots, and on swimming pool covers.

➤ Fix holes in screens so mosquitoes don't join you inside.

LAWN

LAWN CARE

    Watering schedule: _____

    Date fertilized: _____

    Date reseeded: _____

    Date weed killer applied: _____

    Date insecticide applied: _____

SET IN STONE

Rocks have been around since the dawn of time, but they're now more popular than ever in garden designs. Not only are they beautiful, they also solve problems. A few tips:

➤ Does your garden have areas that flood? Rocks help keep your feet dry.

➤ No need to avoid slippery slopes—just add slab steps.

➤ Make a path so strollers—and visitors—can move easily (and stay off your grass).

Plants, Shrubs, and Trees

Your garden is your oasis of calm in a busy, busy world. But do you know what's in it? Here's a handy way to help you remember what you've planted and where, how much you've planted, where to get more, and how to care for what you've got. Keep track of the shrubs and trees in your yard this way, too.

PLANTS
ANNUALS

NAME	HOW MANY	LOCATION	DATE PLANTED	CARE	SUPPLIER

BULBS

NAME	HOW MANY	LOCATION	DATE PLANTED	CARE	SUPPLIER

WELCOME HOME

Add interest to your front porch by surrounding the edges with flowerbeds. Add different shapes and sizes of planters—filled with colorful flowers—to the porch itself for extra height, depth, and beauty.

NATURE AS NURTURE

A Cornell University study recently revealed that children often experience less stress if they can see trees and plants from their windows.

PERENNIALS

NAME	HOW MANY	LOCATION	DATE PLANTED	CARE	SUPPLIER

VEGETABLES

NAME	HOW MANY	LOCATION	DATE PLANTED	CARE	SUPPLIER

DECORATE THE GREAT OUTDOORS

Pretty up your garden with fun and fanciful decorative stakes. You can find stakes topped with metal butterflies, shiny glass prisms, or even ceramic teacups. The endless variety means you'll find one that suits you—and your garden—perfectly.

SHRUBS

NAME	HOW MANY	LOCATION	DATE PLANTED	CARE	SUPPLIER

TREES

NAME	HOW MANY	LOCATION	DATE PLANTED	CARE	SUPPLIER

Notes

Notes

Finances

Finances

Keeping track of your financial information is essential. You can make sound financial decisions only when you know where your money is, how much you have, and what you owe. You need quick and easy access to your financial statements. You also need to remember when to pay your taxes—federal, state, property, and so on—as well as your mortgage payment, insurance payments, and retirement contributions. If your head is spinning, you'll be pleased to know you can record all that information, and more, in this section. You can also record here contact information for the financial professionals and services in your life, like your accountant and your credit card companies, though you should record your credit card numbers and expiration dates elsewhere for security purposes. (For details, *see Passwords and Account Numbers, page 186.*) You'll also find a handy place to keep track of your investments and a clear table that tells you when to keep financial information and when to discard it. Finally, you can use the pocket in this section to hold your latest bank statement, copies of your credit cards (in case they're lost or stolen), and business cards from financial professionals.

Your Financial Life

CONTACT INFORMATION

ACCOUNTANT/TAX ADVISOR: _____

    Phone number: _____ Fax number: _____

    E-mail address: _____

    Address: _____

BANK: _____

    Branch phone number: _____

    Customer service phone number: _____

    Fax number: _____ E-mail address: _____

    Address: _____

    Type of account: _____

BANK: _____

    Branch phone number: _____

    Customer service phone number: _____

    Fax number: _____ E-mail address: _____

    Address: _____

    Type of account: _____

BROKER: _____

    Phone number: _____

    Fax number: _____ E-mail address: _____

    Address: _____

CREDIT BUREAUS

    Equifax: 800-685-1111

    Experian: 888-397-3742

    Trans Union: 800-888-4213

CREDIT CARD/CHARGE CARD COMPANY: _____

    Customer service phone number: _____

    Address: _____

    Annual fee: _____

CREDIT CARD/CHARGE CARD COMPANY: _____

    Customer service phone number: _____

    Address: _____

    Annual fee: _____

CREDIT CARD/CHARGE CARD COMPANY: _____

    Customer service phone number: _____

    Address: _____

    Annual fee: _____

CREDIT CARD/CHARGE CARD COMPANY: _____

    Customer service phone number: _____

    Address: _____

    Annual fee: _____

IDENTITY THEFT . . . FOR THE VERY YOUNG

Identity theft is a large and growing problem, and we're all aware of the basic steps we should take to protect ourselves: Shred unneeded papers that list financial information or your Social Security number; carefully check your credit card statements; and get your credit reports from the large credit bureaus. But did you know that you also have to protect your child's Social Security number to thwart identity thieves? Here's what to do:

➤ Make sure you receive your child's Social Security card a week or two after you apply for it (usually at the hospital where your child was born). If too much time has passed, report the card missing.

➤ Don't give out your child's Social Security number if you can help it. Many schools, camps, and pediatricians request it, but are willing to forgo that information or use an alternate number for identification if you ask.

➤ Contact the Identity Theft Resource Center (858-693-7935 or idtheftcenter.org) if your child starts receiving lots of mail from financial institutions. His or her identity may have been stolen.

CREDIT CARD/CHARGE CARD COMPANY: _____

    Customer service phone number: _____

    Address: _____

    Annual fee: _____

CREDIT CARD/CHARGE CARD COMPANY: _____

    Customer service phone number: _____

    Address: _____

    Annual fee: _____

FINANCIAL ADVISOR: _____

    Phone number: _____

    Fax number: _____ E-mail address: _____

    Address: _____

INSURANCE AGENCY (CAR): _____

    Agent: _____

    Phone number: _____ Fax number: _____

      Address: _____

      E-mail address: _____

    Policy number: _____

      Date bought: _____ Renewal date: _____

INSURANCE AGENCY (DENTAL): *See Safety and Health, page 21.*

INSURANCE AGENCY (HOME): _____

    Agent: _____

    Phone number: _____ Fax number: _____

      Address: _____

      E-mail address: _____

    Policy number: _____

      Date bought: _____ Renewal date: _____

INSURANCE AGENCY (LIFE): _____

    Agent: _____

    Phone number: _____ Fax number: _____

      Address: _____

      E-mail address: _____

    Policy number: _____

      Date bought: _____ Renewal date: _____

INSURANCE AGENCY (MEDICAL): *See Safety and Health, page 20.*

LAWYER: _____

    Phone number: _____ Fax number: _____

    Address: _____

    E-mail address: _____

LAWYER: _____

    Phone number: _____ Fax number: _____

    Address: _____

    E-mail address: _____

MORTGAGE COMPANY: _____

    Phone number: _____ Fax number: _____

    Address: _____

    E-mail address: _____

    Interest rate: _____

SOCIAL SECURITY ADMINISTRATION: 800-772-1213

OTHER: _____

    Phone number: _____ Fax number: _____

    Address: _____

    E-mail address: _____

OTHER: _____

    Phone number: _____ Fax number: _____

    Address: _____

    E-mail address: _____

FINANCIAL DATES TO REMEMBER

INSURANCE PREMIUMS

CAR INSURANCE COMPANY: _____

    Date paid: _____ Amount: _____

    Policy term: _____

    Method of payment: _____

    Check payable to: _____

DENTAL INSURANCE: _____

    Date paid: _____ Amount: _____

    Policy term: _____

    Method of payment: _____

    Check payable to: _____

HOMEOWNER'S INSURANCE: _____

    Date paid: _____ Amount: _____

    Policy term: _____

    Method of payment: _____

    Check payable to: _____

LIFE INSURANCE: _____

    Date paid: _____ Amount: _____

    Policy term: _____

    Method of payment: _____

    Check payable to: _____

CUT YOUR HOME INSURANCE COSTS

Tired of increasingly expensive home insurance? The following strategies can help you reduce those rising premiums:

➤ Do your homework. Check different companies for a cheaper policy before you automatically renew your current policy. Also, contact several agents; you'll find that they will be able to offer you different options.

➤ Increase your deductible. Raise your deductible from $250 to $1,000, and you can save up to 25 percent on the cost of a typical policy. Assuming you'll make a claim once every eight to ten years (for theft or damage, like most homeowners), you'll come out ahead by choosing a lower premium.

➤ Check into discounts. Some insurance companies offer discounts for nonsmokers, people 55 and over, and when you buy auto and homeowner's insurance at the same time. Ask about other savings.

➤ Invest in an alarm system. You may be able to get a small discount if you put heat, smoke, or burglar alarms in your home, or a larger saving if you install certain sprinkler and fire alarm systems tied to an outside service. Remember, though, that you may not recoup the cost of these more expensive systems for a few years.

MEDICAL INSURANCE: _____

    Dates paid: _____ Amount: _____

    Policy term: _____

    Method of payment: _____

    Check payable to: _____

LOANS

BRIDGE LOAN

    Dates paid: _____ Amount: _____

    Interest rate: _____

    Method of payment: _____

    Check payable to: _____

CAR LOAN/CAR LEASE PAYMENT

    Dates paid: _____ Amount: _____

    Interest rate: _____

    Method of payment: _____

    Check payable to: _____

HOME EQUITY LOAN

Dates paid: _____ Amount: _____

Interest rate: _____

Method of payment: _____

Check payable to: _____

MORTGAGE PAYMENT

Dates paid: _____ Amount: _____

Interest rate: _____

Method of payment: _____

Check payable to: _____

STUDENT LOAN

Dates paid: _____ Amount: _____

Interest rate: _____

Method of payment: _____

Check payable to: _____

OTHER LOAN

Dates paid: _____ Amount: _____

Interest rate: _____

Method of payment: _____

Check payable to: _____

RETIREMENT

RETIREMENT CONTRIBUTION (INCLUDING IRAS AND SEPS)

Type of account: _____

Dates paid: _____ Amount: _____

Method of payment: _____

Check payable to: _____

RETIREMENT CONTRIBUTION (INCLUDING IRAs AND SEPs)

Type of account: _____

Dates paid: _____ Amount: _____

Method of payment: _____

Check payable to: _____

TAXES

PROPERTY TAX PAYMENT

Date paid: _____ Amount: _____

Method of payment: _____

Check payable to: _____

QUARTERLY TAX PAYMENTS / FEDERAL

Dates paid: _____ Amount: _____

Method of payment: _____

Check payable to: _____

QUARTERLY TAX PAYMENTS / STATE

Dates paid: _____ Amount: _____

Method of payment: _____

Check payable to: _____

SCHOOL TAXES

Dates paid: _____ Amount: _____

Method of payment: _____

Check payable to: _____

OTHER TAXES: _____

Dates paid: _____ Amount: _____

Method of payment: _____

Check payable to: _____

OTHER TAXES: _____

    Dates paid: _____ Amount: _____

    Method of payment: _____

    Check payable to: _____

THE PAPERWORK PUZZLE

How long should you keep your financial records? The answer depends on the type of paperwork. Here are general guidelines for what to save and what to toss:

➤ ATM receipts: Keep until you get your monthly bank statements. Balance your checkbook, then toss the receipts.

➤ Bank statements (with checks): Keep for seven years for tax purposes.

➤ Bills: Save indefinitely bills for large purchases such as computers, jewelry, cars, and antiques.

➤ Brokerage and mutual fund statements: Save all purchase and sales slips to determine gains and losses for tax time. Keep your quarterly statements until you receive your annual statements; keep end-of-year statements indefinitely.

➤ Credit card statements: Keep the receipts until you get your monthly bank statements. Discard the receipts if everything matches up. Hold on to your credit card statements for seven years for tax purposes.

➤ Home-related documents: Keep records showing the purchase price, the cost of home improvements, and expenses for buying and selling the home indefinitely, even after your sell your house.

➤ Insurance policies: Hold on to these as long as the policies are still in force.

➤ IRA contributions: Keep these records permanently.

➤ Mortgage bills: Hang on to them for as long as you own your house.

➤ Paycheck stubs: Keep for one year.

➤ Tax returns: Keep your returns—and substantiating records—indefinitely.

➤ Utility and phone bills: Keep for one year. If you take a home-office deduction, keep the bills for seven years.

➤ 401(k) and other retirement plan statements: Keep quarterly statements until you get your annual statement, then discard. Keep the annual statements until you retire or close the retirement plan account.

Tax-time reminders

It's tax time: Do you remember all the deductions you should be taking? Use the following space to record the payments and contributions you make throughout the year that can be deducted on your taxes in April. (Don't forget to deduct the interest on your mortgage payments and student loans as well as state and local taxes. For complete information, contact your tax advisor.) You may want to photocopy these pages so that you can use them in years to come.

Gifts to charity

GIVEN TO	DATE	AMOUNT

EDUCATION SAVINGS PLAN:

Date paid: _____ Amount: _____

INTEREST YOU PAID

Home mortgage: _____

Student loan: _____

Other: _____

Other: _____

JOB EXPENSES

ITEMS/SERVICE	DATE	AMOUNT

MEDICAL AND DENTAL EXPENSES (OTHER THAN ROUTINE MEDICAL CARE)

Date paid: _____ Amount: _____

Date paid: _____ Amount: _____

Date paid: _____ Amount: _____

RETIREMENT CONTRIBUTIONS (INCLUDING IRAS, SEPS, AND OTHER QUALIFIED RETIREMENT PLANS)

Type of account: _____

Date paid: _____ Amount: _____

Account fee: _____

RETIREMENT CONTRIBUTIONS (INCLUDING IRAS, SEPS, AND OTHER QUALIFIED RETIREMENT PLANS)

Type of account: _____

Date paid: _____ Amount: _____

Account fee: _____

TAXES YOU PAID

State: _____

Local: _____

Real estate: _____

Other: _____

OTHER: _____

Date paid: _____ Amount: _____

OTHER: _____

Date paid: _____ Amount: _____

IMPORTANT PAPERS

Both you and someone close to you should know where you keep the following important information (which doesn't include vital papers that you carry with you, like your driver's license). Use this table to note where you keep your papers and any comments you have about them.

TYPE OF PAPER/ DOCUMENT	KEPT WHERE?	COMMENTS
Cemetery plot papers		
Checking and savings account information (canceled checks, deposit slips, phone and wire transfer numbers, extra checks, statements)		
Credit records (bills and receipts, copies of contracts, loan statements and payment books, notification forms for lost or stolen credit cards)		
Employment records (copies of employment contracts, benefits information, pay stubs or statements, resume, Social Security records)		
Estate planning (instructions for survivors, unsigned copies of trusts, other legal documents, and a copy of your will)		Leave the original signed copy of your will with your lawyer and your signed "living will" with your doctor
Health information (insurance records, immunization history, surgery history, insurance forms, phone numbers of insurance companies)		

TYPE OF PAPER/ DOCUMENT	KEPT WHERE?	COMMENTS
Household furnishing and appliance records (warranties, manuals, place and date of purchase, receipts, repair records, serial/model numbers)		
Housing records (copies of lease or rental agreements, property tax records, receipts for home improvements, record of mortgage payments)		
Income tax records (copies of past returns, expenses in current year, records and receipts of income and deductible items, tax forms)		
Insurance records: Auto, health, life, disability, property (policies, copies of claim forms, receipts of payment)		
Investment records (purchase, sale, and reinvestment statements for stocks, bonds, mutual funds, 401(k) plans, 529 plans, IRAs, Keoghs, SEPs, real estate earning statements and transaction slips)		
List of insurance policies and agents		
Military service records		
Mortgage documents, title and deeds for your home and other real estate		

TYPE OF PAPER/ DOCUMENT	KEPT WHERE?	COMMENTS
Motor vehicle information (registration copy, repair and maintenance records)		
Motor vehicle titles and purchase receipts		
Personal records for all household members (adoption, birth, citizenship, death, divorce, and marriage certificates; prenuptial agreements; passports; Social Security numbers)		
Social Security card		
Stock, bond, and mutual fund certificates, and purchase and sales receipts		
Tax assessments and records of home capital improvements		

KEEP TRACK OF YOUR CASH

You work hard for your money, and sometimes you need to put in some effort to keep track of it. Here are five simple ways to keep tabs on your cash:

➤ Call or write each financial institution that holds your money at least once a year to keep your accounts active.

➤ Maintain accurate files and check them annually to make sure they are up-to-date—for your bank accounts, stock holdings, insurance policies, and utility and rent deposits.

➤ Make sure you pay the annual fee for your safe deposit box. States treat delinquent accounts differently, but some auction the contents of an unpaid box after only one year.

➤ In addition to your spouse, tell a family member or close friend where you keep your financial records. (Also use the chart above.)

➤ Tell banks, credit card companies, insurance companies, and all other financial institutions when you change residences—in writing. Be sure to send them moving notices.

SAFE DEPOSIT BOX

SAFE DEPOSIT BOX INFORMATION

Location: _____

_____

Box number: _____

Who has access: _____

_____

Who has key (and where): _____

_____

Contents: _____   _____

_____   _____

_____   _____

_____   _____

_____   _____

_____   _____

_____   _____

_____   _____

_____   _____

_____   _____

_____   _____

_____   _____

_____   _____

_____   _____

_____   _____

_____   _____

_____   _____

_____   _____

_____   _____

_____   _____

Renewal fee: _____ Date due: _____

Notes

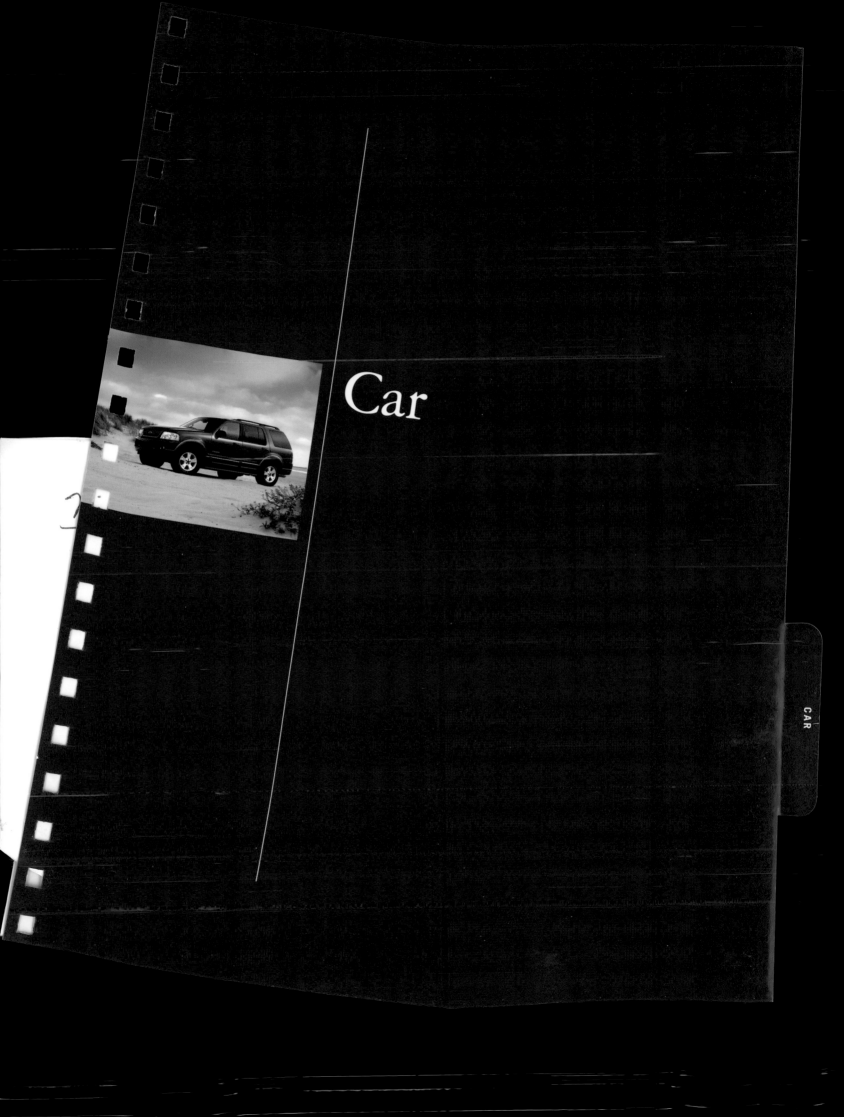

Car

Car

A car can be an integral part of a household, and owning or leasing a car requires attention to details: Keeping your driver's license, registration, and insurance up-to-date; remembering when to take the car in for its annual state inspection; and performing regular maintenance. To ensure your car stays in shape, follow the maintenance schedule in the owner's manual, and record important information about your car in this section; your car will thank you with good service for years to come. Be sure to make copies of your driver's license, registration, and insurance information and store them in the pocket for safety.

Car Care

CONTACT INFORMATION

AUTOMOBILE CLUB: _____

    Roadside assistance phone number: _____

    Other services phone number: _____

    Membership number: _____ Expiration date: _____

DEALER (CAR #1): _____

    Service department

        Phone number: _____ Fax number: _____

        Address: _____

        E-mail address: _____

    Parts department

        Phone number: _____ Fax number: _____

        Address: _____

        E-mail address: _____

    Sales department

        Phone number: _____ Fax number: _____

        Address: _____

        E-mail address: _____

DEALER (CAR #2): _____

    Service department

        Phone number: _____ Fax number: _____

        Address: _____

        E-mail address: _____

    Parts department

        Phone number: _____ Fax number: _____

        Address: _____

E-mail address: _____

Sales department

    Phone number: _____ Fax number: _____

    Address: _____

    E-mail address: _____

DEPARTMENT OF MOTOR VEHICLES

    Phone number: _____ Fax number: _____

    Address: _____

    E-mail address: _____

INSURANCE AGENCY: _____

    Agent: _____

      Phone number: _____ Fax number: _____

      Address: _____

      E-mail address: _____

    Policy number: _____

    Date bought: _____ Renewal date: _____

SERVICE STATION: _____

    Phone number: _____ Fax number: _____

    Address: _____

    E-mail address: _____

GAS TIPS

Try these four tips to stretch your gas dollars:

➤ Fill up at your local wholesale club—you'll generally pay a little less per gallon than at other gas stations.

➤ Check out websites that list gas stations with the lowest prices in your area.

➤ Check your tire pressure frequently. You'll use less gas if your tires are inflated to their recommended pressure. (You can find this information on your car door or in your glove compartment and in your owner's manual.)

➤ Don't use a rooftop carrier on your car. If you use one, you'll decrease your fuel economy by about 5 percent.

OTHER: _____

    Phone number: _____ Fax number: _____

    Address: _____

    E-mail address: _____

OTHER: _____

    Phone number: _____ Fax number: _____

    Address: _____

    E-mail address: _____

DRIVER DETAILS

DRIVER'S LICENSE

    Driver's name: _____

      Number: _____ Expiration date: _____

    Driver's name: _____

      Number: _____ Expiration date: _____

    Driver's name: _____

      Number: _____ Expiration date: _____

CAR #1

    Make: _____

    Model: _____ Year: _____

    License plate number: _____

    Registration number: _____

      Registration expiration date: _____

    Vehicle Identification Number (VIN): _____

    Date purchased: _____ Cost: _____

    Purchased from: _____

      Phone number: _____

      Address: _____

    Mileage at time of purchase: _____

State inspection

    Date inspected: _____

    Place: _____

CAR #2

    Make: _____

    Model: _____ Year: _____

    License plate number: _____

    Registration number: _____

       Registration expiration date: _____

    Vehicle Identification Number (VIN): _____

    Date purchased: _____ Cost: _____

    Purchased from: _____

       Phone number: _____

       Address: _____

    Mileage at time of purchase: _____

    State inspection

       Date inspected: _____

       Place: _____

ELECTRONIC TOLL PASS

    Customer service phone number: _____

    Account number: _____

ELECTRONIC TOLL PASS

    Customer service phone number: _____

    Account number: _____

PARKING PERMIT

    Customer service phone number: _____

    Permit number: _____

    Expiration date: _____ Cost: _____

A KIT FOR THE CAR

Be prepared: It's a good motto for the Boy Scouts and it's a good motto for anyone who drives a car. No matter where you're driving, how long you'll be on the road, or what the weather throws your way, you should keep the following tools, supplies, and documents in your car:

TOOLS TO CARRY
- Flashlight
- Funnel (flexible neck)
- Ice scraper and brush
- Jack
- Jumper cables
- Locking pliers
- Lug wrench
- Penknife
- Pipe (1½ inch diameter, for wrench handle when taking off tire bolts)
- Pliers (adjustable)
- Screwdrivers (slotted blade and Phillips head)
- Shovel
- Tire pressure gauge
- Tow strap or chain
- Wrench set (small)

- Gloves
- Granola bars
- Hand wipes
- Fire extinguisher
- First aid kit
- Flares
- Oil
- Paper towels
- Plastic gallon jugs (empty; to hold water or gas in an emergency)
- Safety glasses
- Sand
- Snow boots
- Spare tire
- Windshield washer fluid
- Wood board (to put under jack on soft ground)

SUPPLIES TO HAVE
- Aerosol de-icer
- Aerosol tire inflator (nonflammable brand)
- Antifreeze (or 50/50 coolant mix)
- Blanket
- Bottled water
- Brake fluid (new, unopened can)
- "Call Police" sign (for window)
- Can opener
- Drive belts (assorted sizes specified for your car model)

DOCUMENTS TO KEEP HANDY
- Auto club membership card
- Credit card or emergency cash
- Driver's license (carry with you)
- Emergency phone numbers
- Insurance ID card
- Maps
- Owner's manual
- Service record or log
- Vehicle registration

PARKING PERMIT

Customer service phone number: _____

Permit number: _____

Expiration date: _____ Cost: _____

For car insurance information, *see Finances, pages 156 and 158.*

For car loan information, *see Finances, page 159.*

MAINTENANCE

CAR #1: _____

Annual tune-up

Date: _____ Place: _____

Phone number: _____ Fax number: _____

Address: _____

Date(s) of oil change: _____
_____
_____

Date(s) tire pressure checked: _____
_____
_____

CAR #2: _____

Annual tune-up

Date: _____ Place: _____

Phone number: _____ Fax number: _____

Address: _____

Date(s) of oil change: _____
_____
_____

Date(s) tire pressure checked: _____
_____
_____

READY, SET, DRIVE!

For easy car maintenance, stock these supplies in your garage:

- Air filter
- Brake fluid
- Funnel with flexible neck
- Motor oil
- Oil filter
- Power-steering fluid
- Transmission fluid

CAR-CARE CALENDAR

Follow this schedule of regular maintenance checks to prevent car trouble. This is a general timetable; for best results, refer to the specific maintenance recommendations and schedule in your owner's manual.

EVERY TIME YOU BUY GAS

☐ Check the engine oil level.

☐ Check the coolant level in the radiator recovery tank.

☐ Check the windshield washer fluid level.

EVERY MONTH OR 1,000 MILES

☐ Check tire pressures.

☐ Examine the tires for tread wear or damage.

☐ Check the surface under your car for leaks when it's parked.

☐ Check the lights.

☐ Check the brake, transmission, and power-steering fluid levels.

EVERY 3 MONTHS OR 3,000 MILES

☐ Change the engine oil and oil filter.

☐ Have the chassis lubricated (if it has lube points).

☐ Check the flashlight batteries in your emergency kit.

EVERY 6 MONTHS OR 6,000 MILES

☐ Check all fluid levels.

☐ Check all drive belts. Adjust any that are loose; replace any that are damaged.

☐ Check all radiator and coolant hoses. Replace any that are damaged or leaking.

☐ Check the battery.

☐ Check the exhaust system for rustouts and leaks. Have defective parts replaced immediately.

ONCE A YEAR OR 15,000 MILES

☐ Have the brakes inspected for damage and wear (twice a year if you do mostly stop-and-go driving).

☐ Change the gas filter.

☐ Check the shock absorbers. Replace any that are leaking or ineffective.

☐ Have the headlight aim checked and adjusted.

☐ Check the air filter.

☐ Have the wheel alignment checked.

☐ Rotate the tires.

☐ Lubricate all hinges and locks.

EVERY 2 YEARS OR 24,000 MILES

☐ Replace the antifreeze.

☐ Have the cooling system flushed if the drained coolant is brown, rusty, or gummy.

☐ Have the timing belt checked (on cars so equipped). Replace it, if necessary.

EVERY 3 YEARS OR 36,000 MILES

☐ Inspect the spark plugs and cables.

☐ Replace cables if they are cracked, brittle, oil soaked, or have soft spots.

☐ Replace worn plugs.

EVERY 4 YEARS OR 48,000 MILES

☐ Replace all drive belts and hoses that haven't previously been replaced.

AS THE SEASONS CHANGE

FOR WINTER

Your car requires special maintenance before cold weather so it will operate smoothly all winter long. Be sure to do the following:

➤ Tune the engine.

➤ Check the battery cables and have a mechanic determine whether the battery itself is fully charged.

➤ Check all lights for working bulbs and clean lenses.

➤ Inspect wipers and washers, and make sure the washer reservoir is filled with fluid that contains windshield washer antifreeze (not engine antifreeze). Put a jug of extra washer fluid in the trunk.

➤ Check defrosters and defoggers.

➤ Rotate the tires.

➤ Have the exhaust system checked. It must be in perfect shape when you drive with the windows closed. The smallest leak in the muffler or exhaust pipes can lead to carbon monoxide poisoning.

➤ Stock your trunk with boots, gloves, an ice scraper and brush, aerosol deicer, jumper cables, a bag of sand, and a small shovel. See *A Kit for the Car, page 176*.

FOR SUMMER

Avoid warm weather problems by preparing ahead of time:

➤ Check all belts and hoses.

➤ Check the antifreeze concentration. If necessary, have the cooling system flushed, the pressure tested, and the thermostat checked.

➤ Have the air-conditioning system tested.

Repair History

Car #1

Make: _____ Model: _____

TYPE OF REPAIR/ REPLACEMENT PART	DATE	COST	SERVICE STATION/ DEALER

CAR #2

Make: _____ Model: _____

TYPE OF REPAIR/ REPLACEMENT PART	DATE	COST	SERVICE STATION/ DEALER

Notes

Passwords
and Account
Numbers

Passwords and Account Numbers

We need to remember an endless number of passwords to get through even an ordinary day. This section gives you the opportunity to record all your passwords, ranging from your alarm company password to your computer passwords to your frequent flyer passwords. You can record important account numbers and your family's Social Security numbers, too. Be sure to photocopy these pages or tear them out of the book, complete them, and store them somewhere extremely secure.

PASSWORDS

ALARM COMPANY PASSWORDS/CODES

Code to enter house: _____

Password for alarm company:_____

ATM/DEBIT CARD PASSWORD:_____

COMPUTER PASSWORDS

Screen name: _____

Password: _____

Screen name: _____

Password: _____

Screen name: _____

Password: _____

Screen name: _____

Password: _____

Screen name: _____

Password: _____

Screen name: _____

Password: _____

CREDIT CARD: _____

Password/personal identification
number: _____

CREDIT CARD: _____

Password/personal identification
number: _____

CREDIT CARD: _____

Password/personal identification
number: _____

CREDIT CARD: _____

Password/personal identification
number: _____

CREDIT CARD: _____

Password/personal identification
number: _____

CREDIT CARD: _____

Password/personal identification
number: _____

FREQUENT FLYER PASSWORDS

Airline: _____

Password: _____

Airline: _____

Password: _____

Airline: _____

Password: _____

GARAGE DOOR PASSWORD: _____

ONLINE BANKING

Bank: _pc financial_

Password: _1 pr 2 in 3 ce_

ONLINE BILL PAYING

Company: _Telus - sballendine_

Password: _prince_

Company: _Bell ExpVu - sballend_

Password: _52 prince 1 PR 2 IN 3 CE_

Company: _hotmail - sballendine_

Password: _~~stuzter~~_

Company: _1 PR 2 IN 3 ce # 52_

Password: _____

Company: _Lowes - saballe_

Password: _1 PR 2 IN 3 ce_
sballendine @ hotmail. com

STORAGE UNIT PASSWORD: _____

WEBSITE PASSWORDS

WEBSITE	PASSWORD
SKYPE sballend	Prince52
TELUS sballend	52 prince
Hotspring decks ↑ sballen ~~sballe~~	52 prince ~Sunroom
Yahoo.ca sballend 52	Pri in 2 ce 3 pet name/pince
bhg.com sballend@telusnet	123 prince
freecycle sballend52@yahoo	pr 1 in 2.ce 3
facebook - sballndrie@hotmail /prince	
Sandy Ball { DAZ 3D - sballndrie@hotmail.com /princeton	
" user name Saballo S/N DS17CRD-0194187-XWU	
Mom ROBSACH3	

TELEPHONE ANSWERING MACHINE

PASSWORD: _____

OTHER: _____
    Password: _____
OTHER: _____
    Password: _____
OTHER: _____
    Password: _____
OTHER: _____
    Password: _____

ACCOUNT NUMBERS

BANK: _____
    Type of account: _____
    Account number: _____
BANK: _____
    Type of account: _____
    Account number: _____
CREDIT CARD: _____
    Account number: _____
    Expiration date: _____

CREDIT CARD: _____

    Account number: _____

    Expiration date: _____

CREDIT CARD: _____

    Account number: _____

    Expiration date: _____

CREDIT CARD: _____

    Account number: _____

    Expiration date: _____

CREDIT CARD: _____

    Account number: _____

    Expiration date: _____

CREDIT CARD: _____

    Account number: _____

    Expiration date: _____

SOCIAL SECURITY NUMBERS

    Name: _____

      Social Security number: _____

    Name: _____

      Social Security number: _____

    Name: _____

      Social Security number: _____

    Name: _____

      Social Security number: _____

    Name: _____

      Social Security number: _____

OTHER FINANCIAL INSTITUTION:

_____

    Type of account: _____

    Account number: _____

OTHER FINANCIAL INSTITUTION:

_____

    Type of account: _____

    Account number: _____

OTHER ACCOUNT NUMBER:

_____

OTHER ACCOUNT NUMBER:

_____

OTHER ACCOUNT NUMBER:

_____

OTHER ACCOUNT NUMBER:

_____

Index